America I AM
LEGENDS

America I AM
LEGENDS
RARE MOMENTS AND INSPIRING WORDS

EDITED BY SMILEYBOOKS

FOREWORD BY TAVIS SMILEY

SMILEYBOOKS

Distributed by Hay House, Inc.

Carlsbad, California • New York City • London • Sydney • Johannesburg • Vancouver • Hong Kong • New Delhi

Copyright © 2009 by Tavis Smiley

Published in the United States by: SmileyBooks, 33 West 19th Street, 4th Floor, New York, NY 10011

Distributed in the United States by: Hay House, Inc.: www.hayhouse.com • *Published and distributed in Australia by:* Hay House Australia Pty. Ltd.: www.hayhouse.com.au • *Published and distributed in the United Kingdom by:* Hay House UK, Ltd.: www.hayhouse.co.uk • *Published and distributed in the Republic of South Africa by:* Hay House SA (Pty), Ltd.: www.hayhouse.co.za • *Distributed in Canada by:* Raincoast: www.raincoast.com • *Published and distributed in India by:* Hay House Publishers India: www.hayhouse.com

Book and Cover Design: Juan Roberts, Creative Lunacy
Front Cover Photo: Michael Ochs Archives/Getty Images

Library of Congress Cataloging-in-Publication Data

America I am legends : rare moments and inspiring words / edited by SmileyBooks ; introduction by Tavis Smiley.
  p. cm.
Includes index.
ISBN 978-1-4019-2410-2 (hardcover : alk. paper) — ISBN 978-1-4019-2405-8 (tradepaper : alk. paper)
1. African Americans—Biography. 2. Successful people—United States—Biography. 3. African Americans—Quotations.
4. African Americans—Quotations, maxims, etc. 5. African Americans—Ethnic identity—Quotations, maxims, etc.
6. Self-realization—United States—Quotations, maxims, etc. 7. Success—United States—Quotations, maxims, etc.
8. Dignity—Quotations, maxims, etc. 9. Inspiration—Quotations, maxims, etc. I. SmileyBooks.
E185.96.A565 2009
920.009296'073—dc22
  [B]
                              200803987

Hardcover: ISBN: 978-1-4019-2410-2
Tradepaper: ISBN: 978-1-4019-2405-8

11 10 09 08 4 3 2 1
1st edition, February 2009

Printed in China

CONTENTS

FANNIE LO

LEGENDS NEVER DIE

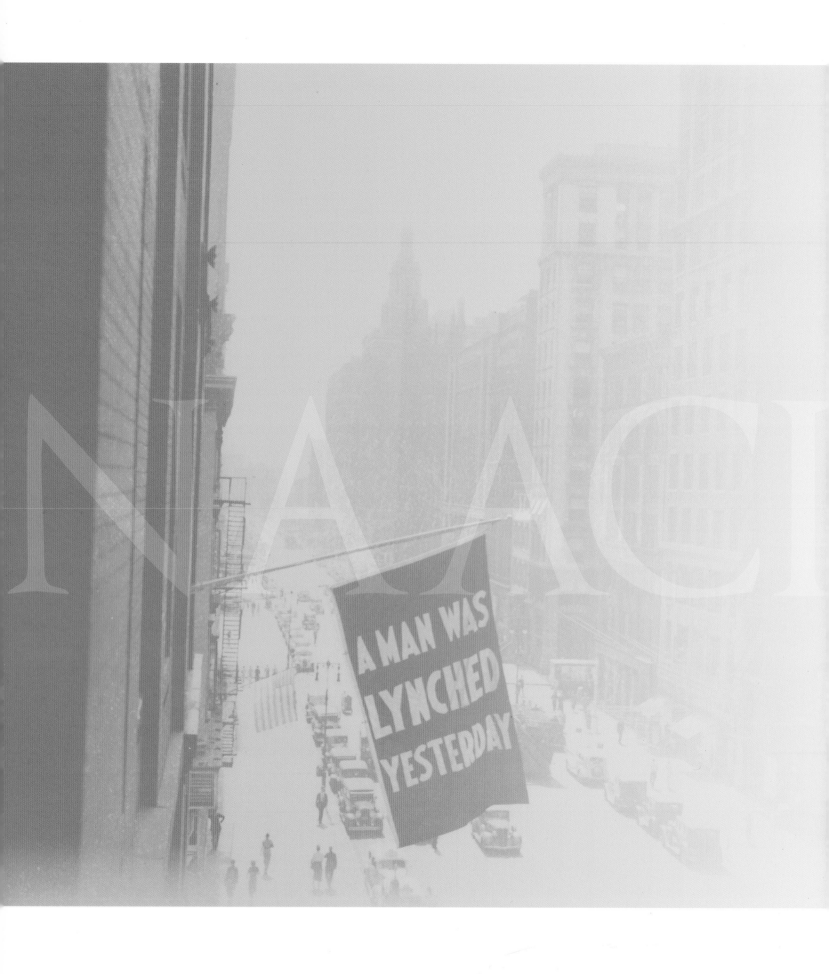

FOREWORD

"WOULD AMERICA HAVE BEEN AMERICA
WITHOUT HER NEGRO PEOPLE?"

—W. E. B. DU BOIS (1903)

W. E. B. Du Bois wrote those words shortly after the turn of the last century. A few decades earlier, a civil war pitted the United States against itself over the status of nearly four million human beings of African descent who were held as slaves. The question came at a time when political and social terrorism against so-called Negroes—including hundreds of lynchings and the villainous social imprisonment of Jim and Jane Crow—had reached a climax. Du Bois rightly predicted that the challenge of the twentieth century would be the color line.

Yet for many, almost unbelievably, here we are in 2008, soaring to unimaginable heights. African American academic, artistic, athletic, political, and social achievements have overcome every obstacle, beating all odds.

THE INDIVIDUAL GENIUS AND COLLECTIVE RESILIENCE OF AFRICAN AMERICAN PEOPLE HAS SHAPED AND NURTURED AMERICAN DEMOCRACY, ENSURING A MORE DIVERSE, SUCCESSFUL, CREATIVE SOCIETY.

More than one hundred years after Du Bois's question was posed, there is only one emphatic and unconditional answer: No! America would not and could not be the America we have come to know—as it is so reverently spoken of in politicians' speeches, as it is presented in our history books—without the deep and inseparable imprint of those people stolen from Africa and brought here on slave ships so many years ago.

No, America would not be America without her Negro people.

When I began work on the America I AM exhibit, I was acutely aware that for something so dynamic and unusual to be successful, it would have to do more than simply relate our history. Through captivating stories, brought to life by brilliant interactive multimedia presentations, we show how our impact on this young nation is essential to the American character—how, in truth, America's story is *our* story. My biggest hope and belief is that, through the America I AM exhibit, we will inspire the younger generation to write the next chapter. Now is the time to prepare our young people to leave their own imprint on America.

Nothing is more inspiring than individual stories of those who struggled head-on against the problems of the twentieth century—and succeeded. It is impossible to think of how we could have accomplished so much, in such a short amount of time, without the abilities, sacrifices, and brilliance of the groundbreakers, the visionaries, and the leaders portrayed in *America I AM Legends*. These seventy-eight extraordinary individuals are our representatives in the gallery of American torchbearers. Each of them shines brightly.

These legends are not the alabaster busts of long-forgotten heroes. They are the living, breathing embodiment of the purpose and power of love. This book is not meant to be the final word, an exclusive club. Deciding who would not be included was excruciating, as volume upon volume could be filled with the stories—our stories—of exceptional abilities, unforgettable contributions, and transformative actions. And this collection still barely scratches the surface of those nameless and faceless heroes who often gave everything trying to make America a nation as good as its promise.

Yet choose we must and choose we did. The bar for legend status is high. Each individual or group must have displayed a transformative ability to weave their gifts and voices into the fabric of America. Take away any of these trailblazers and you have a hole—whether in activism, art, athletics, business, education, music, politics, or spirituality—that no other can fill. The imprint that each of these African Americans has made on the larger cultural landscape has helped shape our nation. The possibilities, opportunities, and expectations of and for greatness that so many of us today have inherited is owed, in large part, to the accomplishments of these forebears.

America I AM Legends is, first and foremost, a celebration. Journey through these pages and you will find stunning images and revealing quotations from an entire century of African American legends. At the beginning, you have the visionary scholar W. E. B. Du Bois. Seen later in life, he bears the noble air of an intellectual giant. Continue and you'll see the musical genius of, among others, Marian Anderson, Chuck Berry, and Prince—musicians who shake the very foundations of American culture. They sit beside the noble work of the NAACP, Ralph Bunche, and Rosa Parks, as they struggle to make the world more just and tolerant. The unparalleled literary genius of Richard Wright, Maya Angelou, and Toni Morrison is undeniable. With them come three generations of American political progress in Shirley Chisholm, Jesse L. Jackson, Sr., and Barack Obama. Open to any page and you'll find a forerunner. Read the accompanying quotes and you will find words that challenge and engage. Delve into the individual Legend Biographies at the conclusion of the book and you'll be amazed at the depth and substance of the lives led. No, America would not be America without her Negro people.

As I sit writing this, I look at images from the time when Du Bois asked his provocative question. The pictures of Black bodies, scorched or hung from trees, or of faded signs hung from storefronts that read "Whites Only," reminds me of how far we have come. We must recognize what courage, what conviction, what commitment it has taken for us to be where we are today. Certainly, the people in this collection provide more than enough inspiration.

Yet look at the still-decimated city of New Orleans. Or at our schools, which have become early entry programs for a schools-to-jail nightmare. Or at our communities, held captive by a seemingly perpetual "economic downturn." Or in our hospitals and community centers, fighting to do ever more with ever less. Look around and you will see a promise unfulfilled.

Unfulfilled but not unfulfillable. Ours has always been a struggle based on hope. We are not fooled or bamboozled by the lure of cheap optimism. We have always known that the path to victory can be paved with unimaginable sacrifice or unwarranted suffering. But it has been this hope—expressed by W. E. B. Du Bois and righteously pursued by Martin Luther King, Jr.—that has provided us the deep steeling of heart, nerve, and spine to move forward, to keep the faith. While we contemplate the lives of those in this book, it is essential that we recognize the moments of pure joy, realized as each unique gift was impressed upon the world, and that for each of these legends, their contribution will remain with us always.

When King declared, "We shall overcome," he was responding sixty-some years later to the challenges and question posed by Du Bois. The dawn of the twenty-first century has seen old rules and assumptions crumble in the face of new challenges and uncertainties, no less daunting than those faced by Du Bois and King in their day. Yet we cannot turn back the hands of time.

And so we now stand at a crossroads. What path will we take? Where will it lead us? How will we change the world along the way? While the answers to these questions remain uncertain, it will only be through deep contemplation and connection with those who faced similar circumstances in times just as turbulent as our own that we will find enough guidance, wisdom, and strength to begin dreaming and building a world of our own choosing.

Through the grand examples set by those presented in *America I AM Legends*, we hope to inspire a new generation to continue forward into the ever-changing, always-developing story that is America. We challenge them to love and serve, to prepare themselves to leave their own indelible imprint upon the world.

—TAVIS SMILEY
September 2008

"WOULD AMERICA HAVE BEEN AMERICA WITHOUT HER NEGRO PEOPLE?"

—W. E. B. DU BOIS

"MY ROOTS ARE IN THE

Corbis

Corbis

BLUES,

IN THE STREET PEOPLE
WHOSE LIVES ARE FULL OF BEAUTY,
AND MISERY, AND PAIN AND HOPE."

—ALVIN AILEY

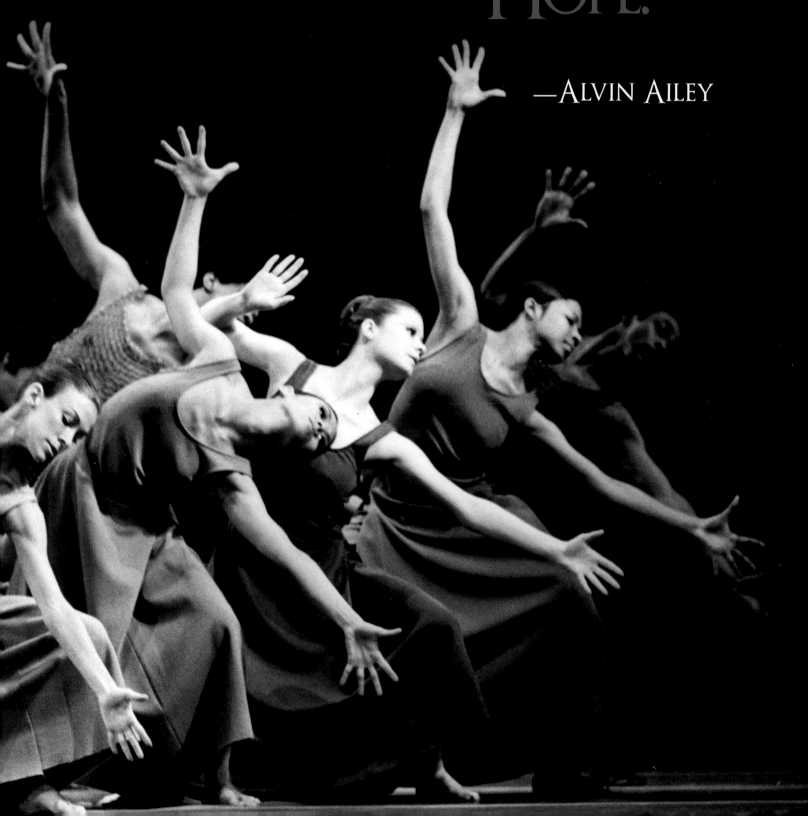

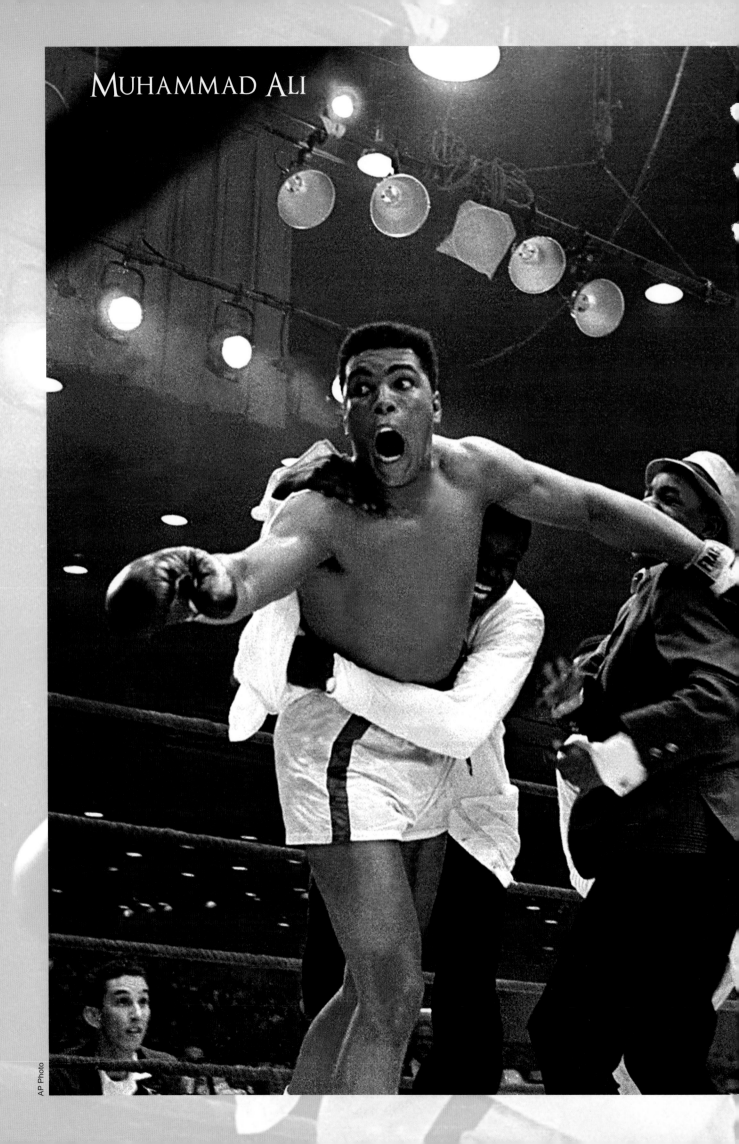

MUHAMMAD ALI

"The embodiment of all of it, the PERFECT machine, the wit, the INCREDIBLE athlete, the facile, ARTICULATE, SHARP MIND on issues, the GREAT SENSE OF HUMOR…"

—HARRY BELAFONTE

"ELLISON
IS THE WRITER THAT
other BLACK
WRITERS
FELT . . . THEY HAD TO BE."

—CHARLES JOHNSON

RALPH ELLISON

"LOUIS ARMSTRONG
IS QUITE SIMPLY
THE MOST IMPORTANT PERSON
IN AMERICAN MUSIC.

HE IS TO 20TH
CENTURY MUSIC...
WHAT EINSTEIN
IS TO PHYSICS."

—KEN BURNS

"IF I DIE,
IT WILL BE IN A GOOD CAUSE.
I'VE BEEN

FIGHTING *for*
AMERICA."

—MEDGAR EVERS

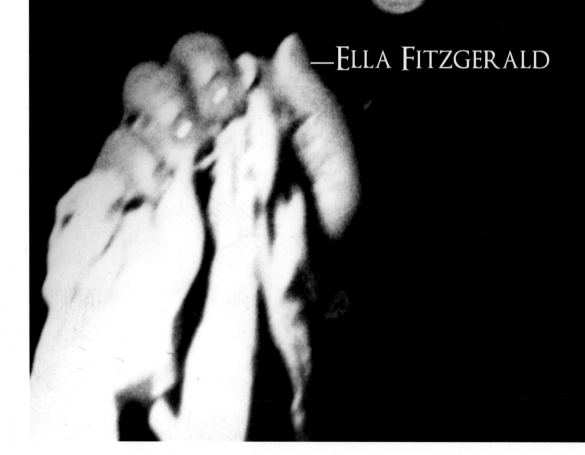

"I GUESS
WHAT EVERYONE WANTS
MORE THAN ANYTHING ELSE IS TO
be LOVED.
AND TO KNOW THAT YOU LOVED ME
FOR MY SINGING
IS TOO MUCH FOR ME."

—ELLA FITZGERALD

13

Michael Ochs Archives/Getty Images

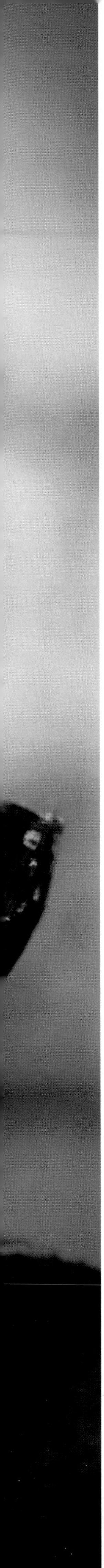

"THE BIGGEST RESULT *of*

WHAT'S GOING ON...

HAD TO DO WITH

MY OWN FREEDOM.

I'D EARNED IT, AND

NO ONE COULD TAKE IT AWAY FROM ME."

—MARVIN GAYE

Michael Ochs Archives/Getty Images

18

"I WISH THEY'D HAD ELECTRIC GUITARS IN COTTON FIELDS

BACK IN THE GOOD OLD DAYS. A WHOLE LOT OF THINGS WOULD'VE BEEN STRAIGHTENED OUT."

—JIMI HENDRIX

"WOMEN,

I BELIEVE THAT YOU MUST BECOME ITS SOUL."

—CORETTA SCOTT KING

21

"BLUES

IS THE BEDROCK OF EVERYTHING I DO.

All of the Characters in my plays, their Ideas and their Attitudes, the Stance they adopt in the world, are all ideas and attitudes Expressed in the Blues."

—August Wilson

"IF I'M GOING *to* SING LIKE SOMEONE ELSE, THEN I DON'T NEED TO SING AT ALL."

—BILLIE HOLIDAY

"HE WAS A SUPER HERO —AN ATHLETE ... A SINGER, AN ACTOR, AND OF COURSE A FIGHTER FOR THE CAUSE of FREEDOM."

—OSSIE DAVIS

PAUL ROBESON

28

"There is
No Greater Agony
than bearing an
Untold Story
Inside
You."

—Maya Angelou

"MOTOWN IS THE GREATEST MUSICAL EVENT THAT EVER HAPPENED IN THE HISTORY OF MUSIC."

—SMOKEY ROBINSON

"WE STUCK TO WHO
WE WERE AT MOTOWN,

and the WORLD CAME AROUND."

—BERRY GORDY, JR.

34

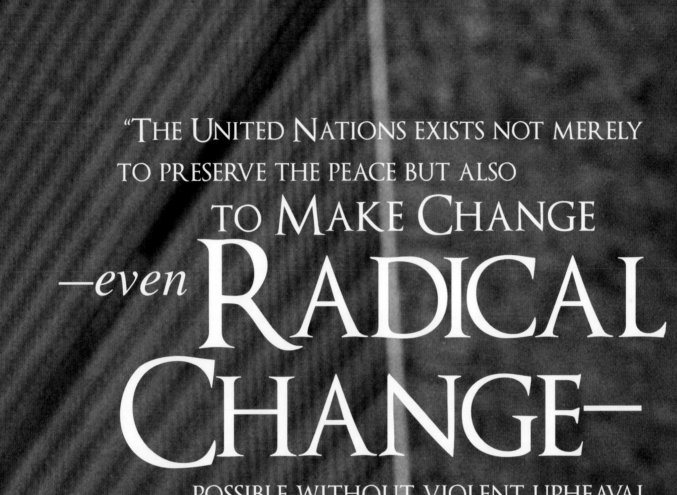

"The United Nations exists not merely to preserve the peace but also to make change —even RADICAL CHANGE— possible without violent upheaval. The United Nations has no vested interest in the status quo."

—Ralph Bunche

"Dreamers march to a Different Beat

because with their third ear they hear something Unordinary ...

David Hume Kennerly/Getty Images News

they DREAM
WITH THEIR EYES OPEN.
THEY ARE THE STUFF
OF WHICH CHANGE IS MADE."

—JESSE L. JACKSON, SR.

"The NAACP... has helped to
WASH AND REWASH
the rather sooty face
of American democracy
and make that face
Cleaner and Brighter
and Better
to look upon
for All Its
Citizens."

—Langston Hughes

"ALEX HALEY'S TAKING
US BACK THROUGH TIME
TO THE VILLAGE OF HIS ANCESTORS
IS AN ACT OF FAITH AND COURAGE,
BUT…ALSO AN

ACT *of*
LOVE…"

—JAMES BALDWIN

"[MALCOLM X] DID NOT CONSIDER HIMSELF TO BE THEIR SAVIOR, HE WAS FAR TOO MODEST *for* THAT, AND GAVE THAT ROLE TO ANOTHER, BUT HE CONSIDERED HIMSELF TO BE THEIR SERVANT AND, IN ORDER NOT TO BETRAY THEIR TRUST, HE WAS WILLING TO DIE."

—JAMES BALDWIN

"THAT JIM BROWN.
HE SAYS HE ISN'T SUPERMAN.
WHAT HE REALLY MEANS IS THAT
SUPERMAN
ISN'T JIMMY BROWN!"

—UNKNOWN NFL PLAYER

"AN INCISIVE DRAMATIST, A CONJUGATOR of SOUL, SHE GETS INSIDE LYRICS AND SHAPES THEM INTO EXTENSIONS OF HERSELF."

—NAT HENTOFF

ARETHA FRANKLIN

"HE ASKS FORBIDDEN QUESTIONS, UNRAVELS SECRET CODES OF RACISM, BRINGS THE GHOST OUT of THE BOX."

—JULIA WRIGHT

RICHARD WRIGHT

"WRONG IS RIGHT."

—THELONIOUS MONK

Ron Sherman/Photoshelter

"I RAN BECAUSE
SOMEBODY HAD TO DO IT
FIRST.
I RAN BECAUSE MOST PEOPLE
THOUGHT THE COUNTRY WAS NOT READY
FOR A BLACK CANDIDATE,
NOT READY FOR A
WOMAN CANDIDATE."

—SHIRLEY CHISHOLM

"I DO NOT BELONG TO THE SOBBING SCHOOL OF

NEGROHOOD

WHO HOLD THAT NATURE
SOMEHOW HAS GIVEN THEM A

LOW DOWN DIRTY DEAL...

NO, I DO NOT WEEP AT THE WORLD
—I AM TOO BUSY
SHARPENING
MY OYSTER
KNIFE."

—ZORA NEALE HURSTON

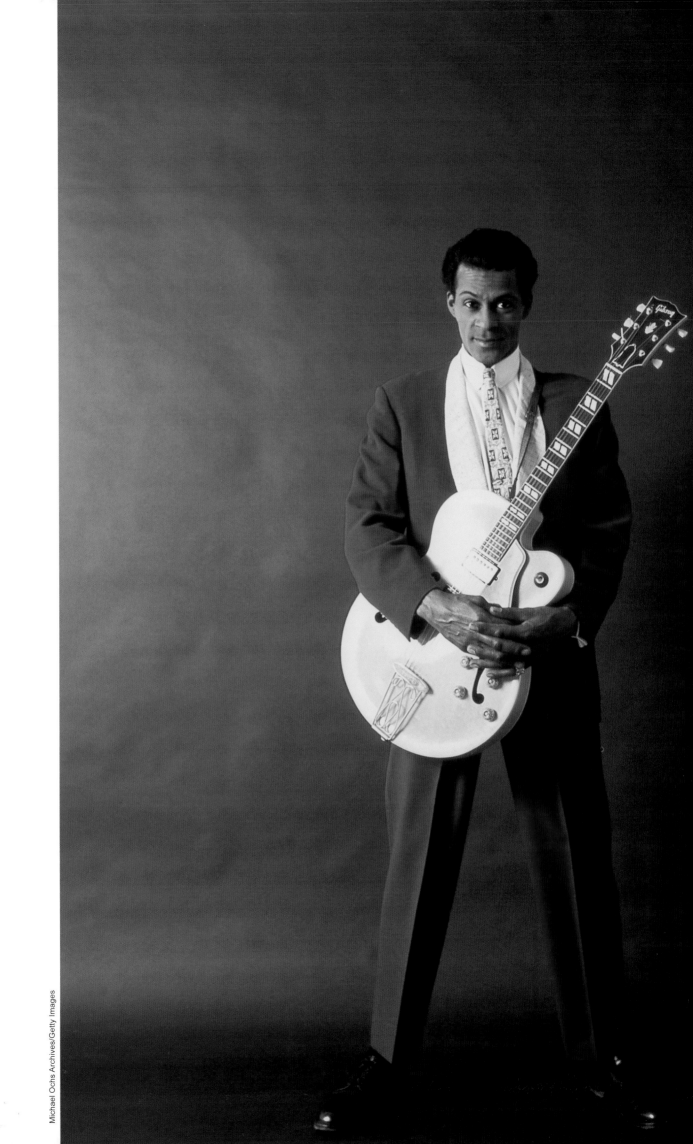

"THERE'S ONLY ONE TRUE KING *of* ROCK 'N' ROLL. HIS NAME IS CHUCK BERRY."

—STEVIE WONDER

"HE REPORTED, CRITICIZED, MADE BEAUTIFUL, ANALYZED, CAJOLED, LYRICIZED, ATTACKED, SANG, MADE US THINK, MADE US BETTER, MADE US CONSCIOUSLY HUMAN."

—AMIRI BARAKA

AP Photo

"MUSIC IS MY GOD."

—NINA SIMONE

"IF THE
HOUSE IS TO BE
SET IN ORDER,
ONE CANNOT BEGIN WITH
THE PRESENT; HE
MUST BEGIN
WITH THE
PAST."

—JOHN HOPE FRANKLIN

ARTHUR ASHE

"ASHE WAS A RARER KIND OF HERO, AN EXAMPLE OF WHAT TO DO WHEN PLAYING STOPS; *a* ROLE MODEL *for* ADULTS."

—S. L. PRICE

"HISTORY TELLS A PEOPLE WHERE THEY STILL MUST GO AND WHAT THEY STILL MUST BE."

—JOHN HENRIK CLARKE

"YOU SAW HER AND YOU GOT THE IDEA

JACKIE JOYNER-KERSEE

OF WHAT A WOMAN ATHLETE
SHOULD BE.

AT THE TIME
IT SEEMED ALMOST LIKE
SHE WASN'T RESPONSIBLE
FOR JUST HER SPORT, BUT
FOR ALL of
WOMEN'S
SPORT."

—MIA HAMM

"I LOVED THE WAY CHARLIE PARKER JUST

FLEW ALL OVER THAT HORN.

THERE AIN'T BUT A FEW NOTES, BUT LOOK LIKE HE ADDED A FEW MORE TO ME."

—SARAH VAUGHAN

"RICHARD PRYOR WAS
THE ROSA PARKS OF COMEDY.
HE TOOK RISKS AND CHANCES THAT
MADE IT POSSIBLE FOR
A WHOLE GENERATION
OF COMICS TO EXIST.
NO ONE EVER
ROCKED
the MIKE
LIKE RICHARD PRYOR."

—CHRIS ROCK

"THE DEPTH
OF HER RESPONSIVENESS
AND HER RANGE
OF POETIC RESOURCES
MAKE HER
ONE OF THE MOST
DISTINGUISHED
POETS
TO APPEAR IN AMERICA
DURING THE
20TH CENTURY."

—GEORGE E. KENT

"WHEN MY COUNTRY, AMERICA, SCREAMED AT ME, TELLING ME I'M A NOBODY, HE GAVE US HOPE."

—SAMUEL PROCTOR

ADAM CLAYTON POWELL, JR.

"JOHN COLTRANE IS STILL PROBABLY ONE OF THE GREATEST MUSICIANS OF THE CENTURY…

WHEN HE STARTS A SOLO WITH HIS SAXOPHONE, IT ACTUALLY SOUNDS LIKE HIS HEART IS MADE OUT OF LIGHT, AND IT IS COMING OUT OF THE HORN… COLTRANE HAS COME THE CLOSEST TO CONNECTING THE ALPHA *to the* OMEGA THROUGH SOUND."

—CARLOS SANTANA

"OUR DESTINY IS BOUND UP WITH

THE DESTINY
of
AMERICA

… WE FEEL THAT WE ARE
THE CONSCIENCE OF AMERICA; WE ARE ITS
TROUBLED SOUL."

—MARTIN LUTHER KING, JR.

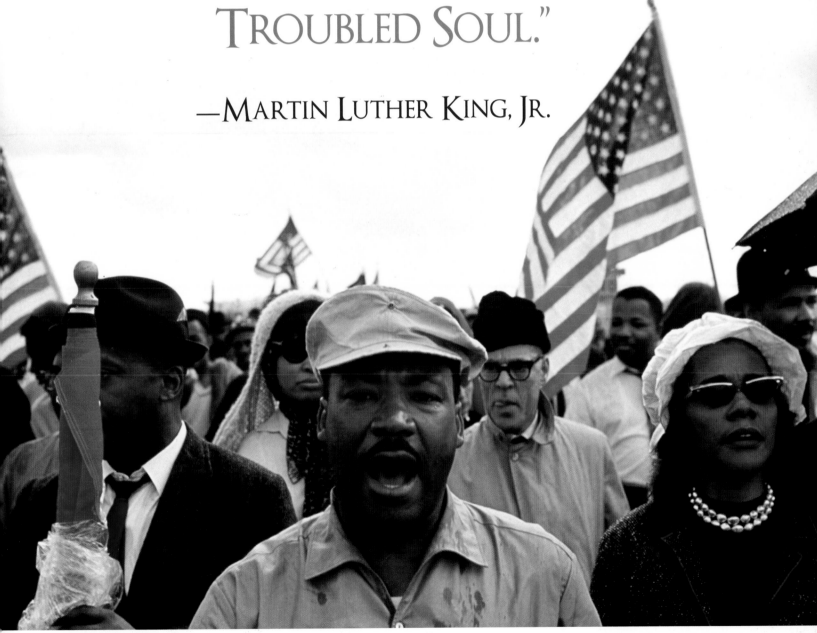

"IT IS MOST IMPORTANT
FOR AN ARTIST TO DEVELOP
AN APPROACH AND
PHILOSOPHY ABOUT LIFE
— IF HE HAS DEVELOPED THIS PHILOSOPHY
HE DOES NOT PUT PAINT ON CANVAS,
HE PUTS
HIMSELF
ON CANVAS."

—JACOB LAWRENCE

"I DON'T KNOW THE KEY TO SUCCESS, BUT THE KEY TO FAILURE IS TRYING TO PLEASE EVERYBODY."

—BILL COSBY

RAY CHARLES

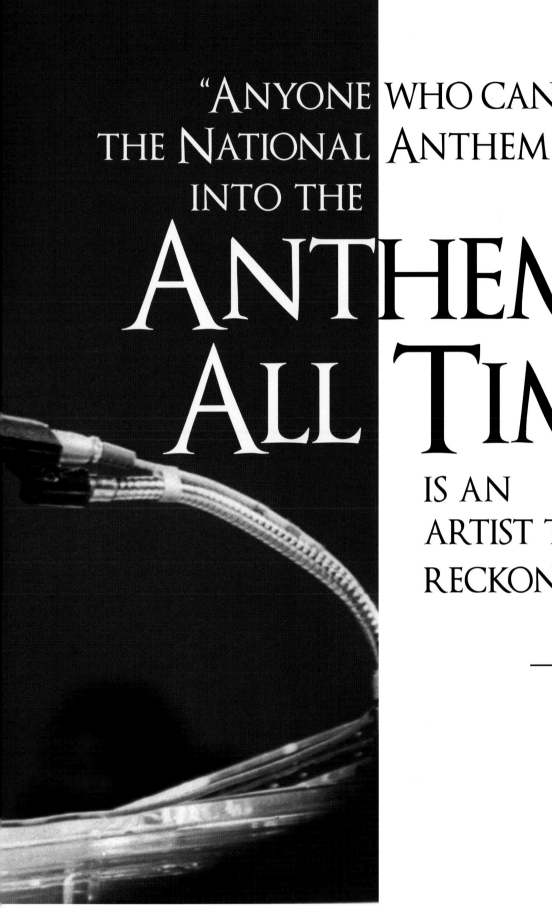

"ANYONE WHO CAN TURN THE NATIONAL ANTHEM INTO THE ANTHEM *of* ALL TIMES IS AN ARTIST TO BE RECKONED WITH."

—NATALIE COLE

"There's Michael Jordan and then there is the rest of us."

—Magic Johnson

"It was
something that just
had to be done.
I don't think I had much to say
in choosing it.
I think
Music
Chose
Me."

—Marian Anderson

"WATCH MICHAEL DANCE

AND YOU'LL UNDERSTAND WHY I'D RATHER BE SINGING WHILE SITTING ON A STOOL."

—MARVIN GAYE

MICHAEL JACKSON

"I RAISED MY VOICE IN **PROTEST AS A MAN** . . . I DIDN'T DO WHAT I DID AS AN ATHLETE."

—JOHN CARLOS

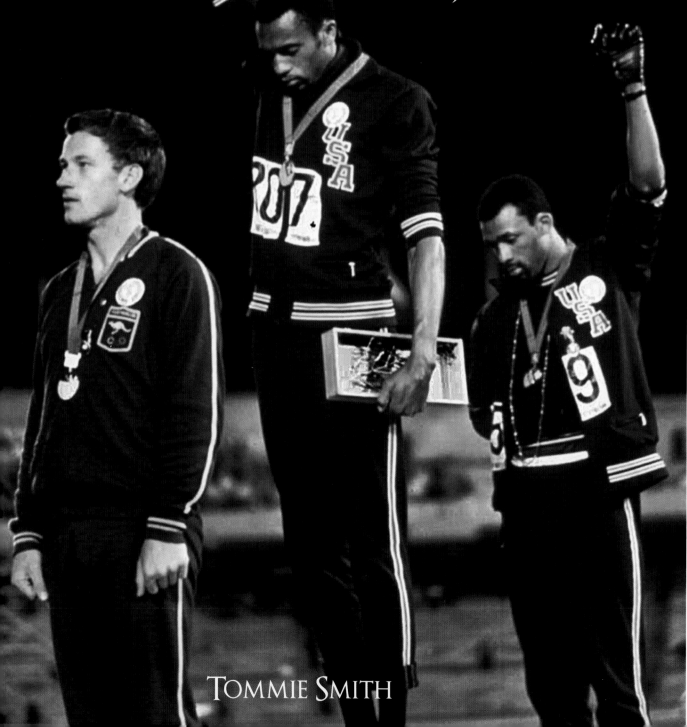

TOMMIE SMITH

JOHN CARLOS

"WE WERE THERE TO
STAND UP
FOR HUMAN RIGHTS
AND TO STAND UP FOR BLACK AMERICANS.
WE WANTED TO MAKE THEM BETTER
IN THE UNITED STATES."

—TOMMIE SMITH

97

"ALICE WALKER TAKES HER READERS INTO FORMERLY TABOO TERRITORY...

SHE INSISTS THAT WE LOOK AT WHAT WE WOULD RATHER PRETEND DOESN'T EXIST; THAT WE HEAR WHAT WE WANT TO CLOSE OUR EARS TO."

—TINA MCELROY ANSA

"I AM JUST ONE NOTE IN A CHORD THAT MAKES A HARMONIC SOUND THAT GIVES ME THE SENSE OF

WHAT I MUST DO
AND WHERE I MUST GO."

—HARRY BELAFONTE

"Only a handful of men and women leave an IMPRINT on the CONSCIENCE of a NATION and on the HISTORY that they helped shape. John Johnson was one of these men."

—Barack Obama

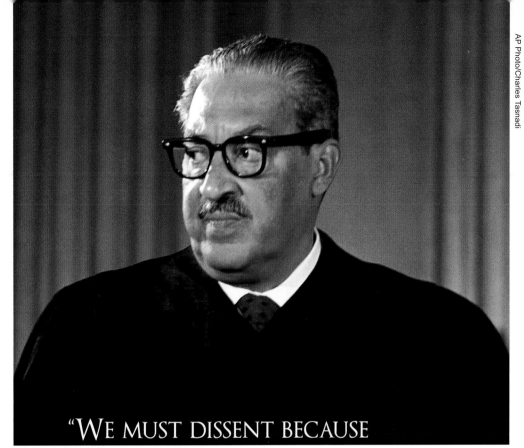

"WE MUST DISSENT BECAUSE

AMERICA CAN DO BETTER,

BECAUSE AMERICA HAS NO CHOICE BUT TO DO BETTER. TAKE A CHANCE, WON'T YOU? KNOCK DOWN THE FENCES THAT DIVIDE. TEAR APART THE WALLS THAT IMPRISON. REACH OUT; FREEDOM LIES JUST ON THE OTHER SIDE."

—THURGOOD MARSHALL

ROMARE BEARDEN

"ROMARE MADE IT SEEM SO SIMPLE,
SO EASY. WHAT I SAW WAS

BLACK LIFE

PRESENTED

ON ITS OWN TERMS,

ON A GRAND AND EPIC SCALE,

WITH ALL ITS

RICHNESS AND FULLNESS,

IN A LANGUAGE THAT WAS

VIBRANT."

—AUGUST WILSON

"ALL MUSICIANS SHOULD GET DOWN ON THEIR KNEES ONCE A YEAR AND THANK THE LORD

John Pratt/Hulton Archive/Getty Images

for DUKE ELLINGTON."

—MILES DAVIS

"JUDGING FROM REACTIONS,
THE **DANCING** OF MY GROUP IS CALLED
ANTHROPOLOGY
IN NEW HAVEN,
SEX IN BOSTON
AND IN ROME—
ART!"

—KATHERINE DUNHAM

"I'M ALWAYS at HOME

BECAUSE I'M THE SAME PERSON
NO MATTER WHERE I AM.
I'M THE SAME PERSON
AT SOME HOLLYWOOD DINNER
THAT I WAS WHEN I WAS BEING HASSLED
BY THE COPS IN MIAMI
OR SLEEPING IN A PAY TOILET
IN NEW YORK."

—SIDNEY POITIER

Corbis

113

"My Mama always used to tell me: 'If you can't find Somethin' to Live for, you best Find Somethin' to Die for.'"

—Tupac Shakur

FIFTY CENTS

AUGUST 11, 1967

"You've got to give us some victories."

TIME

THE WEEKLY NEWSMAGAZINE

Boris Chaliapin

URBAN
LEAGUE'S
WHITNEY
YOUNG

VOL. 90 NO. 6

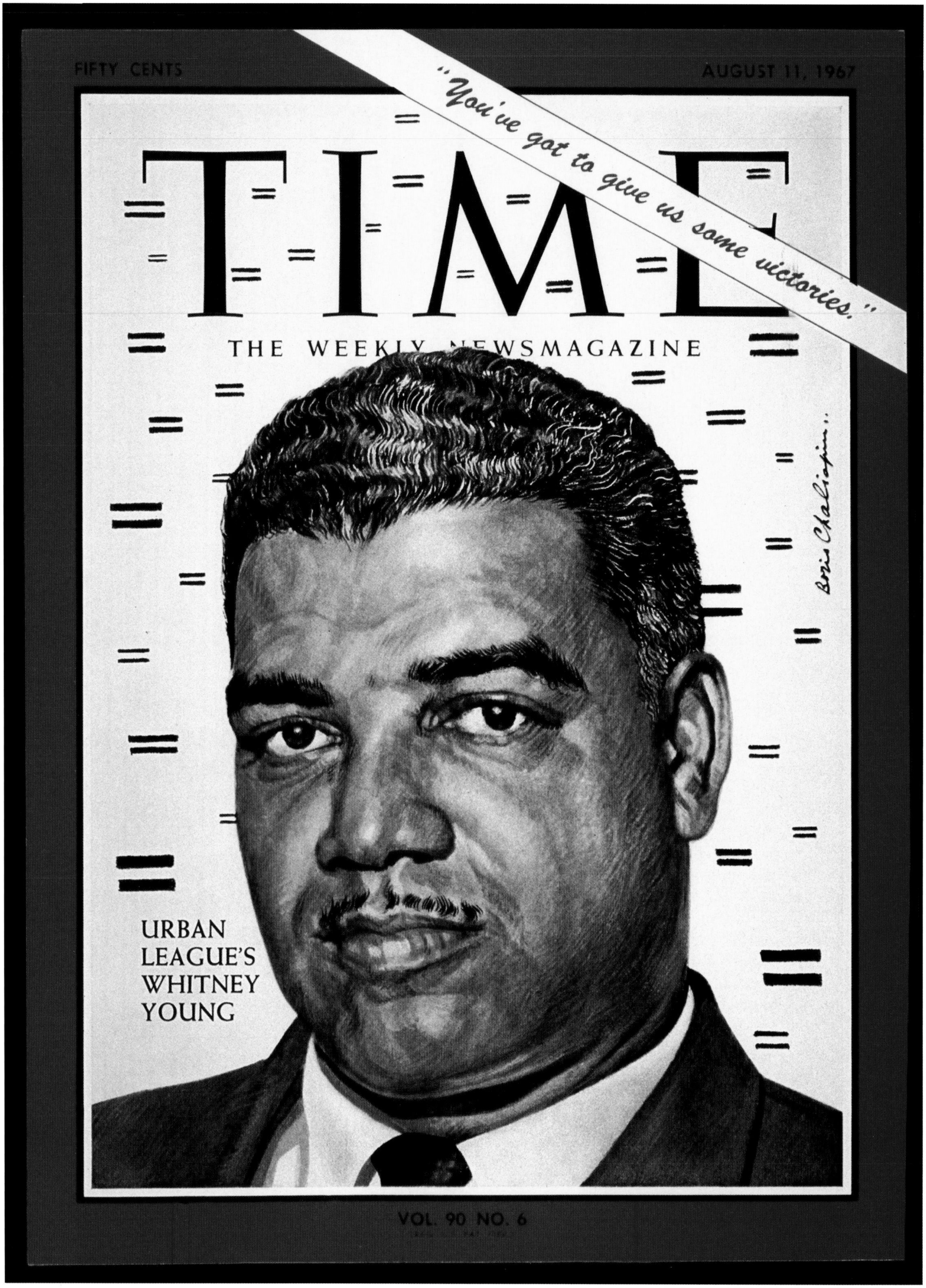

"You can HOLLER, PROTEST, MARCH, PICKET AND DEMONSTRATE, but somebody must be able to sit in on the STRATEGY conferences and PLOT A COURSE."

—Whitney M. Young, Jr.

118

"I BUILT A MAGAZINE TO TEACH THE **BLACK ENTREPRENEUR** HOW TO TAP INTO THE BILLIONS OF DOLLARS WE GENERATE.

That's **BLACK POWER.**"

—EARL G. GRAVES, SR.

"He didn't have **TO SMILE** at everyone, didn't have **TO TELL NO JOKES...** didn't have to say **THANK YOU** or **EVEN BOW.**

HE FIGURED HE COULD JUST

LET THE MUSIC SPEAK *for* HIM

AND FOR ITSELF."

—DIZZY GILLESPIE

MILES DAVIS

"THEIRS IS ONE OF THE MOST
PHENOMEN

AP Photo/Francois Mori

AP Photo/Adam Butler

AP Photo/Richard Drew

TENNIS IS
NEVER MORE EXCITING
OR COMBUSTIBLE THAN WHEN VENUS
AND SERENA ARE IN THE MIX, EITHER
BATTLING EACH OTHER
OR FIGHTING OFF THE PACK."

—WILLIAM C. RHODEN

TONI MORRISON

"THE INDELIBLE WORD PORTRAITS... THE EXPLORATION OF THE PSYCHOLOGICAL TRAUMA OF SLAVERY, RACISM, AND WAR, AND THE SHEER BEAUTY *of* PROSE THAT FREQUENTLY READS LIKE POETRY HAVE ASSURED MORRISON A PLACE IN THE CANON OF WORLD LITERATURE."

—TRUDIER HARRIS

QUINCY JONES

"IN THE
TOTALITY OF HIS TALENT
AND IN HIS DARING
TO BREAK DOWN BARRIERS
and MOVE
ACROSS
BOUNDARIES,
JONES MAY... BE ONE OF THE
MOST INNOVATIVE
PEOPLE IN THE HISTORY
of AMERICAN POPULAR MUSIC."

—GERALD EARLY

"PEOPLE ALWAYS SAY THAT
I DIDN'T GIVE UP MY SEAT BECAUSE I WAS TIRED,
BUT THAT ISN'T TRUE.
I WAS NOT TIRED PHYSICALLY... NO,
THE ONLY TIRED I WAS,
TIRED of
GIVING IN."

—ROSA PARKS

"MAN, WHEN SARAH SANG,
I SWOONED.
I EMULATED HER LUSH LICKS,
HER TASTY TURNS,
HER JAZZ JUMPS,
HER INCREDIBLE RANGE . . .
NO WONDER THEY CALLED HER
the DIVINE
ONE."

—SMOKEY ROBINSON

SARAH VAUGHAN

"HIS TALENT IS

COSMIC...

I THANK GOD FOR STEVIE'S

GIFT

AND THE PRIVILEGE

OF FEELING HIS ENERGY

AT SUCH

CLOSE RANGE."

—MARVIN GAYE

STEVIE
WONDER

"HUGHES SEEMS TO HAVE SET OUT TO TAKE POETRY OFF THE PAGE AND TOSS IT UP INTO THE AIR WE BREATHE; HE DESIRED TO BRING POETRY INTO OUR DAILY LIVES."

—YUSEF KOMUNYAKAA

LANGSTON HUGHES

"I SAW THAT THE
CAMERA
COULD BE A
WEAPON

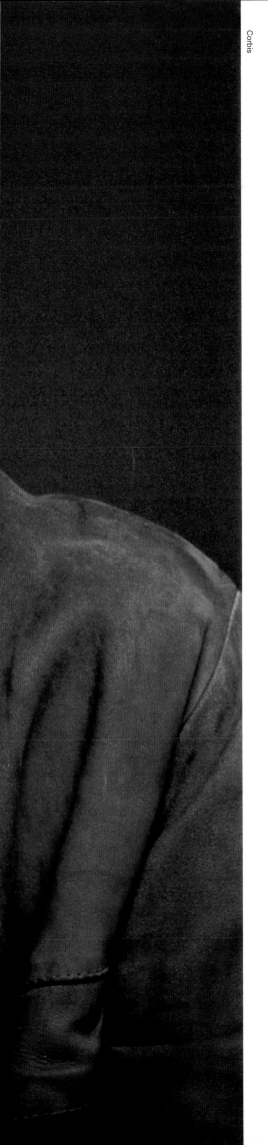

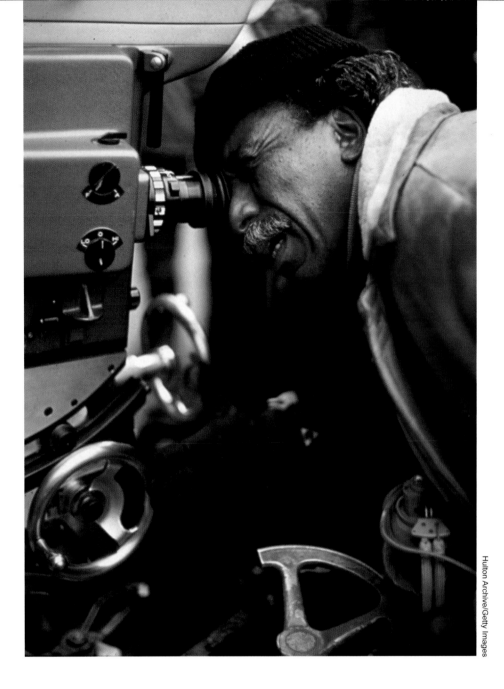

AGAINST POVERTY,
AGAINST RACISM,
AGAINST ALL SORTS OF
SOCIAL WRONGS."

—GORDON PARKS

"I WAS RAISED TO BELIEVE THAT

EXCELLENCE

IS THE BEST DETERRENT
TO RACISM OR SEXISM.

AND THAT'S
HOW I OPERATE MY LIFE."

—OPRAH WINFREY

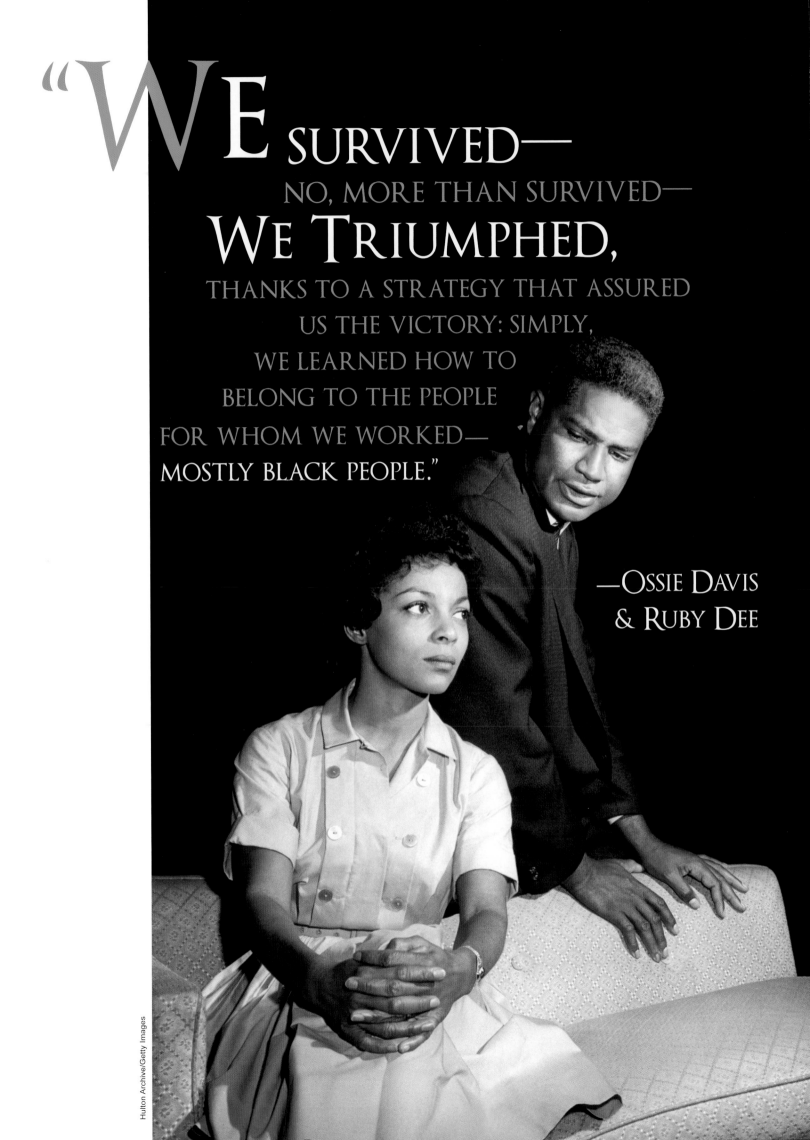

"WE SURVIVED—
NO, MORE THAN SURVIVED—
WE TRIUMPHED,
THANKS TO A STRATEGY THAT ASSURED
US THE VICTORY: SIMPLY,
WE LEARNED HOW TO
BELONG TO THE PEOPLE
FOR WHOM WE WORKED—
MOSTLY BLACK PEOPLE."

—OSSIE DAVIS
& RUBY DEE

"Seldom has one man done so much in so short a time. Seldom has

One Nation

owed so much to One Person."

—Senator Edward Kennedy

JACKIE ROBINSON

"Golf around the world *is* Tiger Woods."

—Thomas Bjorn

"PRINCE...

HE DIDN'T NEED TO BE MACHO.
HE DIDN'T NEED TO BE STREET.
HE CERTAINLY DIDN'T... 'REPRESENT'...

HE SIMPLY
AND EMPHATICALLY
REPRESENTED
HIMSELF."

—BARRY WALTERS

148

"TO TELL *the* TRUTH

TODAY IS TO RUN THE RISK OF BEING KILLED. BUT IF I FALL, I'LL FALL FIVE FEET FOUR INCHES FORWARD IN THE FIGHT FOR FREEDOM."

—FANNIE LOU HAMER

BARACK OBAMA

"THIS OPPORTUNITY FOR A NATIONAL EVOLUTION *(EVEN REVOLUTION)* WILL NOT COME AGAIN SOON, AND I AM CONVINCED YOU ARE *the* PERSON TO CAPTURE IT."

— TONI MORRISON

The Imprint: Legend Biographies

Alvin Ailey (1931–1989): Alvin Ailey's artistic genius was revealed in brilliant choreography that depicted African American life with such poignancy and power that it redefined modern American dance. In 1949, Ailey began to study with choreographer Lester Horton in America's first racially integrated dance company. After Horton's sudden death in 1953, the outstanding twenty-three-year-old talent became the company's artistic director. The following year, Ailey made his Broadway debut in Truman Capote's 1954 *House of Flowers* and remained in New York to study dance with icon Martha Graham.

The Alvin Ailey American Dance Theater (AAADT) made its New York debut in March 1958. Its founder's distinctive fusion of ballet, jazz, African and Cuban dance, and the Dunham technique reflected his unique gifts. Ailey's first major piece, *Blues Suite* (1958), met with wide critical acclaim, but it was *Revelations* (1960), the internationally recognized masterpiece, that launched Ailey and his company to stardom.

In 1965, Judith Jamison joined AAADT as principal dancer. Her graceful, dazzling execution of *Cry* and *Pas De Duke* continued to elevate the company's reputation. Over the next decades, Ailey's creativity as both a dancer and a choreographer advanced professional dance in America, bringing new and established talent together to perform pieces that took the dance world by storm. Ailey was awarded the NAACP Spingarn Medal in 1979 and was a Kennedy Center Honoree in 1988. Upon Ailey's death in 1989, Jamison became the company's artistic director. In 2008, AAADT celebrated its fiftieth anniversary and has performed for an estimated 21 million people around the globe.

Muhammad Ali (b. 1942): Born in Louisville, Kentucky, Cassius Clay became "the Greatest" heavyweight boxer the sport has ever known. He began boxing in junior high, and by 1959 he had become Golden Gloves heavyweight champion and a gold medalist at the 1960 Summer Olympics.

As a professional boxer, Clay stunned opponents with his lightning reflexes, fistic power, speed, and lyrical bravado. In 1964, his shocking defeat of Sonny Liston made him heavyweight champion of the world. Clay fought all newcomers, defending his title nine times. However, the Vietnam War ended his victory streak. In 1964, Clay changed his name and joined the Nation of Islam. In 1967 he refused military induction on religious grounds. The government charged him with draft evasion, stripped him of all titles, and forbade him to box.

In 1971, when the U.S. Supreme Court overturned the original draft evasion decision and ruled that Ali could again box, "The Fight of the Century" between Ali and defending champ Joe Frazier unfolded in New York City. The contest was evenly matched until Frazier put Ali down in the fifteenth round. Ali returned to the ring, fighting all opponents in his weight class until, in 1974, he bested Frazier for the title. That same year, millions watched Ali knock out George Foreman in Zaire's "Rumble in the Jungle." Ali retired in 1982 when diagnosed with Parkinson's disease. In 1996, this international champion stirred crowds around the world as he lit the Olympic flame at the Atlanta summer games.

Marian Anderson (1897–1993): Born in Philadelphia, Marian Anderson used her golden contralto voice to overcome prejudice and fight for artistic freedom in America's concert halls. Anderson began performing at her Baptist church and, in 1919, at age twenty-two, she sang at the National Baptist Convention.

Shortly thereafter, Anderson began touring Black churches and colleges. In 1924 her manager mounted an unsuccessful concert for her at Town Hall in New York City. Anderson, however, refused to give up and entered a competition at the Lewisohn Stadium. She won a prized spot with the New York Philharmonic Orchestra. In 1928, she gave an astonishing solo recital at Carnegie Hall and continued to soar, touring concert halls in Europe. In 1935, Anderson returned to appreciative audiences at Town Hall and Carnegie Hall, and continued her world tour.

Despite these outstanding achievements, in 1939 the Daughters of the American Revolution barred Anderson from performing at Washington, D.C.'s Constitution Hall because of her race. Defiantly, Anderson performed a free open-air concert at the Lincoln Memorial before seventy-five thousand fans and millions of listeners. She began her concert with her trademark quiet grace and dignity, singing "My Country, 'Tis of Thee." Six years later, she sang at the hall that had prohibited her performance. In 1963, she sang at the March on Washington at the request of Martin Luther King and was awarded the Presidential Medal of Freedom.

Maya Angelou (b. 1928): Born Marguerite Johnson in St. Louis, Maya Angelou is the consummate Renaissance woman, with tremendous accomplishments in poetry, letters, dance, theater, film, education, and politics. A survivor of a traumatic childhood, Angelou became a stage performer in the 1950s, working with dance pioneers Martha Graham and Alvin Ailey.

In the early 1960s, Angelou's political consciousness grew as she worked alongside activists, writers, and artists committed to the civil rights movement, including Martin Luther King. She would later live in Egypt and Ghana, working as an editor and journalist. After Dr. King's death in 1968, she wrote her acclaimed memoir *I Know Why the Caged Bird Sings* (1969), which was nominated for a National Book Award. Her volume of poetry *Just Give Me a Cool Drink of Water 'Fore I Diiie* was nominated for the Pulitzer Prize in 1971. She made her Broadway debut in the play *Look Away* in 1973. That same year, she earned an Emmy nomination for her outstanding performance in the groundbreaking TV miniseries *Roots*.

Angelou has published seven memoirs, sixteen volumes of verse, five books of essays, six children's books, ten plays, and four screenplays—all of which have paved the way for other African American writers. A popular performer, educator, and lecturer, Angelou considers her recitation of her poem "On the Pulse of Morning" at the inauguration of President Bill Clinton in 1993 as one of her crowning achievements.

Louis Armstrong (1901–1971): Born in the Storyville District of New Orleans, Louis Armstrong was one of the true geniuses of modern jazz, swing music, and vocal styling. Generations of musicians and singers worldwide are heirs to his trumpet virtuosity, his gravel-voiced vocal stylings, and his introduction of jazz into the mainstream of world music. As a child, Armstrong was sent to the New Orleans Colored Waifs' Home for Boys, and mentored by a musical instructor who taught him the art of playing cornet and singing. By seventeen, he was performing with the top city and riverboat bands, but when he heard his idol, King Oliver, play with Kid Ory's band, he was inspired to seek out the musical path that would define his life.

Armstrong joined Oliver's Creole Jazz Band in Chicago in 1922, but by 1924 he had surpassed his idol and formed his own band, the Hot Five. Their first album debuted in 1925, featuring the classic "St. Louis Blues," with Bessie Smith. As the Depression hit, he felt the pull of swing and founded a bigger band, touring across the States and Europe. During the war years and beyond, Armstrong developed into the consummate entertainer, appearing on radio, in films, and on television. In the '50s and '60s, Armstrong was recognized as an international jazz original, performing classics like "Ain't Misbehavin'," "Mack the Knife," and "Hello Dolly." Armstrong's passion for his music also fueled his work as America's goodwill ambassador in Africa and around the world.

Arthur Ashe (1943–1993): Born in Richmond, Virginia, tennis champion and celebrated humanitarian Arthur Ashe blazed trails in world tennis as the first African American man to win a Wimbledon title and induction into the International Tennis Hall of Fame. His innate talent was discovered early on the public courts of Richmond and cultivated by outstanding coaches. This led to the development of his masterful skills as an aggressive player on the UCLA tennis team. Although he faced racism throughout his career (1969–1980), he never let such obstacles deter him; rather, they seemed to motivate him to use his fame as a platform.

In the late 1960s and 1970s, on the world professional tennis circuit, Ashe was twice ranked No. 1 in men's tennis. While a member of the U.S. Davis Cup team, he suffered a heart attack and was forced into early retirement. Nevertheless, he stayed involved in the game he loved as a sports commentator and inner-city tennis program advocate. He was also a vocal and compelling presence in the South African antiapartheid movement. In 1988, after his diagnosis of HIV resulting from a tainted blood transfusion administered during heart bypass surgery, he became a champion for HIV/AIDS education and research. Ashe's unique legacy as an extraordinary role model on and off the court lives on in his three-volume history of Black athletes, *A Hard Road to Glory* (1988), and his celebrated *New York Times* bestselling memoir *Days of Grace* (1993).

James Baldwin (1924–1987): Born in Harlem, novelist, essayist, playwright, and activist James Baldwin was a peerless critic of racial and social inequality, religious hypocrisy, and sexual oppression. After leaving home at age seventeen, Baldwin worked odd jobs until he began writing full-time in 1943. Publishers rejected his early work, yet he persisted, cultivating his craft by writing reviews and essays for elite White magazines, eventually winning a Rosenwald Fellowship in 1948.

Baldwin's first novel, *Go Tell It on the Mountain* (1953), and his first collection of essays, *Notes of a Native Son* (1955), launched an outstanding and prolific writing career. He followed with *Giovanni's Room* (1956), *Nobody Knows My Name* (1961), and *The Fire Next Time* (1963), offering a brilliant examination of race in America. In the wake of America's growing civil unrest, Baldwin became a vigorous social activist who challenged the status quo, never hesitating to raise his pen in the quest for racial equality. Friend and adviser to civil rights leaders such as Martin Luther King, Stokely Carmichael, and Malcolm X in the 1950s and 1960s, Baldwin marched, spoke at fund-raisers, and stood firmly for social change. Throughout his life, Baldwin's fearless voice sparked national debate on racism and injustice, and has inspired generations of writers around the world.

Romare Bearden (1911–1988): A profound influence on American art, music, performing arts, and art education, Romare Bearden was born in Charlotte, North Carolina. He followed his dream of becoming an artist through his education at Lincoln University, Boston University, and New York University. After graduation, he continued to explore his passion at the Art Students League in New York City and later at the Sorbonne in Paris. For nearly three decades, Bearden turned his extraordinary talents into the creation of literally thousands of works in multiple mediums—collages, watercolors, oils, and photomontages—while keeping his full-time job as a civil servant.

Bearden enjoyed creative associations with some of the most esteemed artists, musicians, and entertainers of his time. In 1964, he was the first art director of the Harlem Cultural Council and was a key supporter in the development of African American art institutions, such as the Studio Museum and the Cinque Gallery. His impressive literary contributions include *The Painter's Mind*, coauthored with Carl Holty (1969), *Six Black Masters of American Art*, coauthored with Harry Henderson (1972), *The Caribbean Poetry of Derek Walcott and the Art of Romare Bearden* (1983), and *A History of African-American Artists: From 1792 to the Present* (1993). A founding member of the Black Academy of Arts and Letters in 1970, he was inducted into the National Institute of Arts and Letters in 1972. Today, Bearden's art is exhibited in leading galleries and in private collections the world over.

Harry Belafonte (b. 1927): Award-winning entertainer and internationally acclaimed social activist and humanitarian, Harry Belafonte was born in Harlem. He helped put Caribbean style on the musical map and has been an indefatigable defender of human rights around the world.

Belafonte's musical career began as a pop singer in 1949, but he quickly turned to folk music and released his 1953 classic, "Matilda," followed by his 1956 million-copy album *Calypso* with RCA Victor.

A dedicated and outspoken social activist, Belafonte was an early supporter of the civil rights movement. In the 1950s he provided financial support to Martin Luther King's family, and later financed the Freedom Rides, bailed Dr. King out of various jails, and helped organize the 1963 March on Washington. During the 1960s, his commitment to world music inspired him to introduce numerous international music artists to American audiences.

After studying acting alongside Marlon Brando and Sidney Poitier, Belafonte performed in such notable films as *Carmen Jones* (1954), *Island in the Sun* (1957), *Odds Against Tomorrow* (1959), *Uptown Saturday Night* (1974), and *Kansas City* (1996).

A lifelong global activist, Belafonte was one of the creators of the "We Are the World" African famine relief effort, the Live Aid concerts, and the 2001 HIV/AIDS campaign in Africa. He has been a goodwill ambassador for UNICEF since 1987 and has received, among many awards, the Kennedy Center Honors (1989), the National Medal of Arts (1994), and the Grammy Lifetime Achievement Award (2000).

Chuck Berry (b. 1926): A native of St. Louis, Chuck Berry—the "Father of Rock and Roll"—transformed contemporary music by marrying Country & Western licks to Rhythm & Blues, perfecting the unique sound and bold moves that became Rock and Roll. His gifts were first revealed in a high school talent show, where he sang a blistering "Confessin' the Blues." That raucous, blues-drenched pop country sound became Berry's trademark and by 1953 he had joined a local band playing the St. Louis Cosmopolitan Club.

In 1955, Berry's own band toured Chicago and dropped into a club where his idol, Muddy Waters, was playing. This blues icon introduced Berry to Leonard Chess, owner of Chess Records, who signed him and produced the hit "Maybellene." Berry's magical connection with adolescent audiences and his dynamic star power helped him to draw racially mixed crowds to his concerts throughout his career, breaking down the doors of Jim Crow entertainment taboos. Between 1957 and 1959, he enjoyed a steady presence high on the pop charts with hits like "Brown Eyed Handsome Man," "Memphis," "Too Much Monkey Business," "Roll Over Beethoven," and "Johnny B. Goode."

The ecstatic energy of his stage show inspired '60s-era bands from the Beatles to the Rolling Stones. Over the decades, Berry's "scorching guitar solos built around his trademark double-string licks," cited by the Rock and Roll Hall of Fame, enshrined him as one of the organization's first inductees in 1986.

Gwendolyn Brooks (1917–2000): The first African American author to win the Pulitzer Prize in any category, Gwendolyn Brooks was born in Topeka, Kansas, and raised in Chicago. Brooks's parents made their daughter the focus of their aspirations. Her parents' ambitions were realized quite unexpectedly when Brooks met two leading Harlem Renaissance poets, James Weldon Johnson and Langston Hughes, who saw her at a high school performance and encouraged her to continue writing. Sharpening her abilities through writing workshops, Brooks wrote three works of verse, including *A Street in Bronzeville* (1945), which gained instant critical acclaim and her first Guggenheim Fellowship. Her next book, *Annie Allen* (1950), won *Poetry* magazine's Eunice Tietjens Prize as well as the 1950 Pulitzer Prize for poetry.

A literary pillar of the Black arts movement in the late 1960s, Brooks made the decision to publish her books with exclusively Black presses in 1969. She received many honors throughout her career, including poet laureate of Illinois (1968), poetry consultant to the Library of Congress (1985), and the National Endowment for the Humanities Jefferson Lecturer (1994). A dedicated educator, she taught at Columbia College (Chicago), Northeastern Illinois University, Elmhurst College, Columbia University, Clay College of New York, and the University of Wisconsin. Over her lifetime, Brooks wrote twenty-two books of poetry, seven books of fiction, several children's books, and a memoir, *Report from Part One: An Autobiography.*

James Brown (1933–2006): Born in Barnwell, South Carolina, James Brown, the "Godfather of Soul," changed the rhythms and tempos of pop, soul, blues, funk, and even hip-hop, with a rocking band, socially conscious lyrics, and often imitated dance moves. Raised by an aunt who ran a brothel in Augusta, Georgia, Brown did odd jobs to survive and at times had run-ins with the law. In 1949, Brown joined Bobby Byrd and the Flames and by 1955 was the band's lead vocalist, recording the million-copy single "Please, Please, Please."

In 1958, Brown's powerful ballad "Try Me" topped the charts. Throughout the '60s and '70s, Brown's desire to reflect Black life in America with no excuses inspired a series of smoking funky tunes that made him an indelible star, such as "Papa's Got a Brand New Bag," "It's a Man's Man's Man's World," "Say It Loud—I'm Black and I'm Proud," and "Sex Machine." Brown's influence even extended to Africa, evident in artists such as King Sunny Ade, Fela Kuti, and Youssou N'Dour.

Brown's songs of Black pride and respect provided the soundtrack for the civil rights movement of the 1960s and 1970s. In 1986, Brown was one of the first artists to be inducted into the Rock and Roll Hall of Fame. He was awarded a Grammy Lifetime Achievement Award in 1992, Kennedy Center Honors in 2003, and a 2003 BET Lifetime Achievement Award.

Jim Brown (b. 1936): Born on St. Simons Island in coastal Georgia, Jim Brown is regarded as one of the National Football League's greatest running backs, as well as a groundbreaking actor and activist. At age eight, Brown moved with his mother to Long Island. While in high school, he earned an extraordinary thirteen letters in sports. College records fell while Brown attended Syracuse University, where he was the team's leading rusher. In his senior year he earned all-American honors, while rushing for three touchdowns and 132 yards during a memorable Cotton Bowl.

In 1957, Brown was chosen as a fullback by the Cleveland Browns in the first round of the draft and was voted into the Pro Bowl every season he played. He retired in 1966 after Browns owner Art Modell demanded he report to training camp instead of finishing his role in *The Dirty Dozen*. Brown left the game with several single-season and career records—in rushing yards, in total touchdowns, and, as an all-time leader, in rushing touchdowns. Over his nine-season professional fullback career, Brown never missed a game. His incredible prowess led to induction into the Pro Football Hall of Fame in 1971.

His films include *Rio Conchos* (1964), *The Dirty Dozen* (1967), *100 Rifles* (1969), *Three the Hard Way* (1974), and *On the Edge* (2001). In 1988, Brown founded an organization dedicated to the rehabilitation of troubled youths, inmates, and gang members—the Amer-I-Can Foundation—which continues today.

Ralph Bunche (1904–1971): Born in Detroit, statesman and social scientist Ralph Bunche spent his life advocating for the right of all humanity to live with mutual respect and in peace.

After the death of his parents, when he was twelve years old, Bunche and his two sisters went to Los Angeles with their grandmother, where he impressed all with his academic brilliance. He attended UCLA on an athletic scholarship and graduated valedictorian with a degree in international relations. He received his master's degree from Harvard University in 1928.

Throughout his career, Bunche was active in educational and civil rights issues. His significant achievements included participation in the noted Carnegie Corporation survey of the American Negro under the guidance of Gunnar Myrdal in 1944; membership in FDR's "Black Cabinet"; organization of the civil rights marches coordinated by Martin Luther King in the 1960s; adviser to the State Department; and leadership in the UN Palestine Commission (June 1947 to August 1949), helping to reach an armistice between Israel and the Arab states. This latter effort won him the NAACP Spingarn Medal (1949) and the Nobel Peace Prize (1950). From 1955 to 1971, Bunche served as United Nations undersecretary for Special Political Affairs and then undersecretary-general. In 1963, he was awarded the Presidential Medal of Freedom.

John Carlos (b. 1945): Harlem native John Carlos was the 1968 Mexico City Summer Olympics track star and founding member of the Olympic Project for Human Rights. A talented high school athlete, Carlos attended East Texas State University on a track scholarship and later went to San Jose State University, where he was mentored by the brilliant track coach Lloyd Winter.

A world-class sprinter, he was the bronze medalist finishing in the Olympic 200-meter finals behind American Tommie Smith and Australian Peter Norman. As Carlos and Smith stood on the podium, they defied Olympic protocol and stunned the world by raising their black-gloved fists, protesting injustice and poverty in America. In the controversy surrounding their protest, Carlos and Smith were suspended from the U.S. team and banned from the Olympic Village. Death threats were made against them.

The next year, Carlos continued to excel in track competitions, equaling the world record in the 100-yard dash in the Amateur Athletic Union (AAU) and guiding San Jose State to its first NCAA championship with wins in the 100 and 200. He was a gold medalist at the 1967 Pan American Games in Canada and smashed all indoor records in the 60-yard and 220-yard dashes. In 2003, Carlos was inducted into the National Track & Field Hall of Fame. In 2005, San Jose State University honored Smith and Carlos with a twenty-two-foot-high statue re-creating their Olympic protest. At the 2008 ESPY Awards ceremony, Smith and Carlos received the Arthur Ashe Courage Award honoring their world-changing political activism.

Stokely Carmichael (1941–1998): Political activist and Pan-Africanist Stokely Carmichael was an international civil rights leader who preached revolutionary Black nationalist philosophy. Born in Port of Spain, Trinidad, Carmichael grew up in Harlem and the Bronx, and later attended Howard University, where he became deeply involved with campus civil rights activities. In 1960, he joined the Student Nonviolent Coordinating Committee (SNCC). While working with SNCC and the Congress of Racial Equality (CORE), Carmichael joined the Freedom Rides to end racist practices in the South. He and his fellow civil rights activists often faced repression and severe abuse—at one point Carmichael spent forty-nine days in Mississippi's infamous Parchman Farm Penitentiary.

The "Freedom Summer" of 1964 gained Carmichael national notice as a dynamic, courageous speaker who helped organize rural Blacks in the South into a strong political force. As a SNCC field organizer in Lowndes County, Alabama, he was credited with helping to increase voter registration from seventy to twenty-six hundred, in a county where the African American majority had no elected representation. In 1966, he replaced future congressman John Lewis as chairman of SNCC in a shift that disturbed many White liberal allies and angered older veterans of the civil rights campaigns. It was that year, at a march in Selma, Alabama, that the mantra "Black Power" was first used. In 1968, Carmichael was named honorary prime minister of the Black Panther Party. The following year, after changing his name to Kwame Ture, he moved to Africa, where he spent the remainder of his life writing, lecturing, and supporting Pan-Africanist philosophy.

Ray Charles (1930–2004): Born in Albany, Georgia, musical genius Ray Charles Robinson was a trendsetting singer and musician who helped bring R&B into the American mainstream. Blinded at age seven, Charles attended the St. Augustine School for the Deaf and the Blind in St. Augustine, Florida, where he honed his musical gifts. In 1947, he moved to

Seattle, where he began recording and playing in bars and clubs. By 1949, Charles's "Confession Blues" had climbed the charts to No. 2. He followed with another hit, "Baby, Let Me Hold Your Hand" in 1951 and signed with Atlantic Records the following year.

During his Atlantic career, Ray Charles produced successful single after single, hit album after album, for the jukebox and the dance floor, including "It Should Have Been Me," "Mess Around," "Drown in My Tears," "Georgia on My Mind," "Hit the Road Jack," and "Unchain My Heart." Despite a drug problem, Charles continued to top the charts, tour for several months out of the year, and make occasional television appearances from 1960 through the 1980s. He performed at two presidential inaugurations—Ronald Reagan's in 1985 and Bill Clinton's in 1993. His band kept a rigorous tour schedule throughout the latter part of his life. He was voted into the Rock and Roll Hall of Fame in 1986, and in the same year he received the Kennedy Center Honors. Winner of over a dozen Grammys, including the Grammy Lifetime Achievement Award in 1987, Charles was inducted to the Rhythm and Blues Foundation in 1991.

Shirley Chisholm (1924–2005): A native of Brooklyn, Shirley Anita St. Hill was the first female African American elected to the U.S. Congress and the first African American to seek her party's nomination for president of the United States. This groundbreaking educator and politician graduated from Brooklyn College in 1946 and was awarded a master's degree in elementary education from Columbia University's Teachers College in 1952.

A passionate advocate for child care and educational issues, Chisholm was an education consultant to the New York City Bureau of Child Welfare in 1959. She became involved in local politics in the late 1950s and 1960s, learning the electoral process from the ground up. Frustrated with the lack of Black legislative representation in 1964, she decided to run for the New York State Assembly, winning by a wide margin. Demanding equality for minorities and women, she was elected to the U.S. Congress in 1968, adding her distinctive voice to that august body.

Her first book, *Unbought and Unbossed* (1970), advanced her themes of integrity and fairness. After running for the 1972 Democratic Party's presidential nomination, she wrote her second book, *The Good Fight* (1973), which sought to bring attention to many social and racial issues inside the Democratic Party. She served in her congressional seat until retiring in 1983. President Clinton selected Chisholm as ambassador to Jamaica in 1993, and she was inducted that same year into the National Women's Hall of Fame.

John Henrik Clarke (1915–1998): Born in Union Springs, Alabama, John Henrik Clarke distinguished himself as a scholar, historian, Black nationalist, and Pan-Africanist. He was one of the most informed, perceptive educators and writers of African and African American history in modern times.

After moving to New York City from Chicago in the 1930s, Clarke—who possessed no formal academic training—began studying the history and role of persons of African descent under Arturo Schomburg. In 1949, Clarke was invited by the New School for Social Research to teach courses at the newly created African Studies Center. He later joined the staff of Hunter College as an associate professor of African and Puerto Rican studies. He was appointed professor emeritus in 1985. Clarke's groundbreaking work inspired Cornell University to name the Africana Center library in his honor in 1985.

Clarke's distinguished publishing credits include many books on Black history, among them *Harlem USA: The Story of a City Within a City* (1964), *Harlem: A Community in Transition* (1964), and *Malcolm X: The Man and His Times* (1969). He coedited *Black Titan: W. E. B. Du Bois* (1970). Excelling in African history, he wrote volumes of brilliant political and cultural analysis, including *Africans at the Crossroads: Notes for an African World Revolution* (1991), *Christopher Columbus and the Afrikan Holocaust* (1992), and *African People in World History* (1991).

John Coltrane (1926–1967): Born in Hamlet, North Carolina, John Coltrane expanded the vocabulary of the jazz saxophone solo and became one of the most influential artists in the evolution of jazz, providing generations of artists and intellectuals with a new champion. Raised in North Carolina, his family moved to Philadelphia in 1943 following his father's death. Two years later, he was drafted into the navy, where he developed as a musician in a navy band.

After his discharge in 1945, he joined bands led by Johnny Hodges and Dizzy Gillespie. In 1955, while working as a freelance musician in Philadelphia, Coltrane received a call from trumpeter Miles Davis, who invited him to join his quintet, launching his dynamic professional career.

Miles put him through his paces during this growth period, producing such masterpieces as "Workin'," "'Round about Midnight," "Milestones," "Kind of Blue," and "Someday My Prince Will Come." But it was the fabled Atlantic and Impulse sessions, with pianist McCoy Tyner, drummer Elvin Jones, and bassists Steve Davis and Jimmy

Garrison, that sealed Coltrane's reputation as a true innovator. The jazz world was mesmerized by Coltrane's new sonic explorations, beginning with the revolutionary recording *Giant Steps* (1959), considered by many to be one of the greatest records of all time. His originality reached new heights with the equally seminal *A Love Supreme* (1964). Coltrane was inducted into the *Down Beat* Jazz Hall of Fame in 1965 and given a posthumous Grammy Lifetime Achievement Award in 1992.

Bill Cosby (b. 1937): Comedian, educator, and philanthropist, Bill Cosby was one of the first African Americans to break down the doors of exclusion in mainstream humor, combining sharp-witted commentaries with an Everyman accessibility that allowed him to gain wide crossover appeal. The son of a navy man, Philadelphia native Cosby joined the service after leaving high school in 1956. In 1961, he entered Temple University on a track scholarship, where he discovered his comedic talents. Cosby took the stage in 1962 at the Gaslight Café in New York City. Eventually getting booked at the Gaslight for sixty dollars a week, he left college to pursue a life in entertainment.

Cosby's lighthearted humor became an instant hit, landing him in the national spotlight with an appearance on *The Tonight Show* in 1963. In 1965, Cosby became the first African American to break into primetime, costarring in the spy-spoof television series *I Spy*. He would win three Emmys before the show ended in 1968.

Throughout the late 1960s and 1970s, Cosby continued to produce hit comedy albums and television shows, including *Fat Albert and the Cosby Kids* (1972–1984). But it was *The Cosby Show*, which first aired in 1984, that would achieve Cosby's highest level of critical and cultural success. As "America's Dad," obstetrician Cliff Huxtable, Cosby presented a wholesome upper-middle-class Black family to millions of viewers, defying the media's pervasive stereotypical portrayal of African Americans. Today, Cosby continues to tour and to devote time to his educational and philanthropic campaigns.

Miles Davis (1926–1991): One of jazz's central figures, Miles Davis continually set new trends, from bebop and mainstream small-band improvisation, to the advent of electric funk and fusion music. Born in Alton, Illinois, the son of a successful dentist, he inherited a passion for music from his mother, who played piano and violin. He was so proficient on trumpet that he played with Eddie Randle's Blue Devils around St. Louis throughout high school.

After high school, Davis enrolled in The Juilliard School of Music, studying during the day and playing his horn at night. In 1945, he joined Charlie Parker's band and made his first record two years later. He brought a new lyricism and a simmering soul to his trumpet work on the famed *Birth of the Cool* (1949). He formed his first legendary quintet in 1955, with bassist Paul Chambers, pianist Red Garland, drummer Philly Joe Jones, and tenor saxophonist John Coltrane. His thirty-year partnership with Columbia Records permitted Davis to experiment with a host of styles from hard bop to orchestral projects, electric funk to ambient sounds, with albums such as *'Round About Midnight* (1955), *Kind of Blue* (1959), *Bitches Brew* (1969), *We Want Miles* (1981), *Miles Under Arrest: Live* (1985), and *Tutu* (1986). Over his illustrious career, Davis earned eight Grammy Awards, the 1984 Sonning Award, and a 2006 induction into the Rock and Roll Hall of Fame.

Ossie Davis (1917–2005): Born and raised in Cogdell, Georgia, Raiford Chatman Davis became an outstanding actor, writer, playwright, and film director who made inestimable contributions to the civil rights struggle and to African American culture. He attended Howard University before pursuing an acting career in New York City. Drafted in 1942, Davis served in the army medical corps and Special Services before being discharged in 1945. After his service, Davis landed a lead role in a New York play, *Jeb*, where he met his future wife, Ruby Dee.

During the McCarthy era, Davis and Dee were blacklisted, named as Communists and racial militants by the House Un-American Activities Committee (HUAC). They took the lead in crucial civil rights protests, becoming friends and advisers to many of the movement's spokespeople, such as Martin Luther King and Malcolm X. Davis was one of the organizers of the 1963 March on Washington, and he delivered the eulogy at Malcolm X's funeral in 1965.

Among Davis's many stage, film, and television credits are *No Way Out* (1950), *The Joe Louis Story* (1953), *Purlie Victorious* (1961), *The Cardinal* (1963), *The Hill* (1965), *Do the Right Thing* (1989), *Jungle Fever* (1991), *Malcolm X* (1992), and *The L Word* (2004). Davis wrote more than twelve plays and directed five films. Although he was proud of winning an Emmy Award in 1963, he felt his long career was truly honored by the NAACP Image Award Hall of Fame (1989) and the Kennedy Center Honors (2004).

Ruby Dee (b. 1924): At age eighty-three, Ruby Dee remains at the forefront of distinguished African American artists and activists, both onstage and in film. Born Ruby Ann Wallace in Cleveland and raised in Harlem, she graduated from Hunter College with degrees in French and Spanish. Dee appeared in roles on Broadway before gaining national acclaim for her performance in the 1950 film *The Jackie Robinson Story*, which launched her movie career.

Her acting history is one of a woman always striving for dignity and pride in her varied roles, including *Edge of the City* (1957), *A Raisin in the Sun* (1961), *Buck and the Preacher* (1972), *Roots: The Next Generation* (1979), *Their Eyes Were Watching God* (2005), and *American Gangster* (2007). She has been nominated for eight Emmy Awards, winning one for her role in the 1990 made-for-TV movie *Decoration Day*. She received a 1971 Obie Award for Best Performance by an Actress for her work in *Boesman and Lena* and a 2001 Screen Actors Guild Lifetime Achievement Award. In 1998, Dee and her husband, Ossie Davis, wrote *With Ossie & Ruby: In This Life Together*, which in 2007 earned them a Grammy Award for Best Spoken Word album. She was also nominated for a 2008 Academy Award for Best Supporting Actress for her role as Mama Lucas in *American Gangster*, for which she won a Screen Actors Guild Award.

W. E. B. Du Bois (1868–1963): Born in Great Barrington, Massachusetts, W. E. B. Du Bois was the most influential Black scholar and intellectual of twentieth-century America. He was educated at Fisk University and Harvard University, where he was the first African American to receive a Ph.D., in 1895. With the publication of *The Souls of Black Folk* in 1903, Du Bois changed the debate on race in America forever. In 1905, he helped organize the Niagara movement, which led to the founding of the National Association for the Advancement of Colored People (NAACP) in 1909.

During the 1920s, Du Bois feuded with Marcus Garvey over the assimilation of Blacks into American society. A decade later, his heralded "Talented Tenth" theory put him at odds with Booker T. Washington, and later with Walter White and Roy Wilkins at the NAACP. He wrote books, memoirs, and novels, including *The Philadelphia Negro* (1899), *John Brown: A Biography* (1909), *The Quest of the Silver Fleece* (1911), *The Negro* (1915), *Black Reconstruction* (1935), and *Black Folk, Then and Now* (1939). Additionally, he assisted in founding four journals, among them the NAACP's *The Crisis* and *Phylon*.

Du Bois visited Communist China and the Soviet Union during the early 1950s and signed the Stockholm peace pledge, which opposed the use of atomic weapons. He was questioned by the House Un-American Activities Committee and was indicted under the Foreign Agents Registration Act, but was acquitted. In 1963, he and his wife became citizens of Ghana, where he died the day before the famous 1963 March on Washington.

Katherine Dunham (1909–2006): Choreographer, anthropologist, and writer, Katherine Dunham was one of America's pioneering dance innovators. Born in Joliet, Illinois, Dunham attended the University of Chicago in the 1930s, majoring in dance and anthropology. In the early 1940s, Dunham founded the Katherine Dunham Company, the first African American modern dance company. She would later go on to found the Katherine Dunham School of Dance in New York in 1945. By the time it closed in 1955, the school had established a lasting legacy for young dancers, some of whom went on to open Dunham Technique schools in Paris, Stockholm, and Rome.

Revered as a performance artist and dancer, she excelled on the Broadway stage and in films, including *Stormy Weather* (1943). Dunham created other works during the war period, such as "Rara-Tonga," "Rites de Passage," and "Plantation Dances," and choreographed hit stage productions, including *Choros* (1944), *Carib Song* (1945), and *Bal Nègre* (1946). Her dance troupe started an international tour in 1947 that lasted more than twenty years, performing throughout Europe, North Africa, South America, Australia, and the Far East.

In 1967, after a show at the Apollo Theatre in Harlem, Dunham retired. She was awarded numerous honors and tributes, including the 1983 Kennedy Center Honors and the 1989 National Medal of Arts Award, as well as ten honorary doctorates.

Duke Ellington (1899–1974): Born in Washington, D.C., Edward Kennedy "Duke" Ellington was arguably America's greatest all-around musician, exerting enormous influence on the concept and content of popular music through his jazz compositions and gifted performances of his big bands. Playing professionally in his teens, by 1924 Ellington's musical fluency had landed him in the vibrant heart of jazz and the Harlem Renaissance. Though his early focus had been on ragtime, the young pianist and composer quickly embraced the dynamic possibilities of jazz. Soon, Ellington's Washingtonian band—featuring some of the greatest early jazz musicians—was regularly showcased at Harlem nightspots, such as the Kentucky Club and the Cotton Club.

By the time Ellington played Carnegie Hall in 1943, his big band sound had brought him fame across the globe. Along with co-composer Billy Strayhorn, Ellington wrote, arranged, and conducted some of the greatest musical pieces of his day, including "Mood Indigo" (1930), "It Don't Mean a Thing (If It Ain't Got That Swing)" (1932), "In a Sentimental Mood" (1935), "Do Nothing Till You Hear from Me" (1940), and "Take the 'A' Train" (written by Billy Strayhorn in 1941). Ellington's impressive performance at the 1956 Newport Jazz Festival landed the composer on the cover of *Time* magazine.

Widely honored, Ellington won thirteen Grammys, the Grammy Lifetime Achievement Award (1955), the Presidential Medal of Freedom (1969), the Legion of Honor (France, 1973), and a Pulitzer Prize Special Citation (1999).

Ralph Ellison (1914–1994):
Born in Oklahoma City, Ralph Ellison's ability to give voice to the struggles facing African Americans in postwar America propelled him to distinguished literary heights and secured his place in the canon of American literature. Musically inclined as a child, Ellison studied at the Tuskegee Institute and dreamed of moving to New York City to work as a musician. Once there, he began to cultivate his writing and was encouragd by such luminaries as Richard Wright. In 1952 Ellison published *Invisible Man*. Its masterfully wrought depiction of the African American experience earned the first-time novelist a National Book Award.

With friends Arna Bontemps, Langston Hughes, Robert Penn Warren, William Styron, and Albert Murray guiding his career, Ellison brought his unique brand of symbolism to two perceptive essay collections: *Shadow and Act* (1964) and *Going to the Territory* (1986). He continued working on a long-awaited second novel after a fire destroyed a sizeable portion of the text. Meanwhile, Ellison taught creative writing at Rutgers University, New York University, and Bard College. Selected awards include a Chevalier of the Ordre des Arts et des Lettres from France, the Medal of Freedom, the National Book Award for Fiction, and the Russwurm Award. Two of Ellison's books were published after his death in 1994: *Flying Home: And Other Stories* (1996) and *Juneteenth* (1999).

Medgar Evers (1925–1963):
Field secretary for the Mississippi NAACP, Medgar Evers was murdered by a member of the Ku Klux Klan for organizing Blacks to register to vote. His death ushered in a new, more urgent era of civil rights activism. Born in Decatur, Mississippi, Evers dropped out of high school at seventeen to join the army, and served in World War II before being honorably discharged in 1945. Later, he attended Alcorn State University, majoring in business administration.

In 1951, he married Myrlie Beasley, whom he met at Alcorn, and the couple moved to Mississippi, where Evers worked with T. R. M. Howard's Magnolia Mutual Life Insurance Company. Howard was also the president of the Regional Council of Negro Leadership, a civil rights group. In 1954, Evers applied to the segregated University of Mississippi Law School and was rejected. He became the subject of an NAACP lawsuit and joined a boycott that desegregated the university when it was forced to enroll James Meredith in 1962.

The increasingly vocal Evers traveled deep into rural Mississippi, speaking out against prejudice, which resulted in numerous death threats. On May 23, 1963, a firebomb was thrown into the carport of his home. Two weeks later, Evers was getting out of his car, carrying T-shirts reading "Jim Crow Must Go," when he was shot in the back. He died at a local hospital almost an hour later. Many regard Evers's untimely death as the tipping point that led President John F. Kennedy to push Congress to pass major civil rights legislation.

Ella Fitzgerald (1917–1996):
Born in Newport News, Virginia, Ella Fitzgerald was one of the most influential virtuoso singers at the height of the jazz era. After her parents' separation, Fitzgerald and her mother moved to Yonkers, New York, where she grew up poor but determined. By 1934, Fitzgerald was selected to sing at the Apollo Theatre amateur night. She would go on to win the first-place prize of twenty-five dollars. Afterward, drummer Chick Webb hired her to travel with his band and soon she recorded her first song, "Love and Kisses," in 1936. Her playful 1938 rendition of "A Tisket, A Tasket" sold one million copies, making Fitzgerald a star at twenty-one. When Chick Webb died in 1939, she took over the band and renamed it Ella Fitzgerald and Her Famous Orchestra.

Throughout the 1940s and '50s, Fitzgerald would tour the world, perform with some of the greatest artists of her day, and record some of the most respected jazz melodies of all time. Some of her unforgettable recordings include: *Pure Ella* (1950), *Ella Fitzgerald Sings the Cole Porter Songbook* (1956), *Ella Fitzgerald Sings the Duke Ellington Songbook* (1957), *Ella Swings Brightly with Nelson* (1962), and *Ella and Basie!* (1963). In 1979, Fitzgerald received the Kennedy Center Honors for lifelong achievement. In 1987, President Reagan awarded her the National Medal of Arts. In 1991, she gave her final concert at Carnegie Hall—her twenty-sixth performance there.

Aretha Franklin (b. 1942): Born in Memphis and raised in Detroit, Aretha Franklin redefined the emotional range of American music with her sheer vocal agility. The daughter of the influential Rev. C. L. Franklin, she sang in her father's church as a girl and recorded her debut album for Columbia Records, *The Gospel Soul of Aretha Franklin*, at the young age of fourteen.

After Franklin's relationship with Columbia became strained she moved to Atlantic Records in 1966, where she was given far more creative control. Her subsequent work there created some of her most commercially successful milestones. Her first single, "I Never Loved a Man the Way I Loved You," stayed at the R&B singles No. 1 spot for seven weeks, paving the way for other successful albums that secured her star status, including *Lady Soul* (1968), *Aretha Now* (1968), *Spirit in the Dark* (1970), *Young, Gifted and Black* (1971), and *La Diva* (1979), her final Atlantic disk.

The African American community responded passionately to Aretha's music, which stressed Black strength and pride along with women's empowerment on such remarkable tracks as "Respect," "Think," "A Natural Woman," and "Chain of Fools." Franklin, unanimously crowned "the Queen of Soul" and the first Black woman to grace the cover of *Time* magazine, has charted forty-five singles in all, more than any other female singer. Franklin was the first woman inducted into the Rock and Roll Hall of Fame in 1987. She is the recipient of many honors, including the Kennedy Center Honors Award (1994) and induction into the NAACP's Hall of Fame (1997).

John Hope Franklin (b. 1915): One of America's foremost historians and scholars, John Hope Franklin contributed crucial research that helped lead to the U.S. Supreme Court's decision to overturn *Brown v. Board of Education*. Born in Rentiesville, Oklahoma, he earned an undergraduate degree from Fisk University in 1935 and a doctorate in history from Harvard University in 1941.

In the 1950s, Franklin was active in the NAACP Legal Defense Fund, under the supervision of Thurgood Marshall, helping litigate *Brown v. Board of Education*. After World War II, he taught at Howard University until his selection to chair the history department at Brooklyn College in 1956—the first person of color to head a major history department. He taught history at the University of Chicago in the 1960s and chaired the department from 1960 to 1970. Franklin was appointed to the U.S. delegation to the United Nations Educational, Scientific and Cultural Organization (UNESCO) General Conference in 1980. In 1983, he was appointed the James B. Duke Professor of History at Duke University, assuming emeritus status in 1985.

A prolific author, he has written several classics pertinent to the African American experience: *From Slavery to Freedom: A History of Negro Americans* (1947), *The Emancipation Proclamation* (1963), *Racial Equality in America* (1976), and a memoir, *Mirror to America: The Autobiography of John Hope Franklin* (2005). He has also been appointed to serve on many national commissions on the humanities and the President's Initiative on Race. In 1995, he was awarded the Presidential Medal of Freedom.

Marvin Gaye (1939–1984): A true American music original, Washington, D.C.–born Marvin Gaye defined the soulful evolution of African American pop music from the 1960s to the 1980s, creating an enduring sound that resonates to this day. Like many, Gaye began his singing career in the church choir. After a brief stint in the air force, he floated from local act to local act until, in 1961, Motown founder Berry Gordy, Jr., signed Gaye as a session drummer and backup singer.

Although his early solo efforts met with mixed reviews, Gaye's creative alliance with Motown helped him land his first Top Ten hit, "Pride and Joy" (1963), a highly popular album, *Together* (1964), and a medley of duets with Mary Wells. From there, the progression of golden '60s singles kept coming: "How Sweet It Is to Be Loved by You," "Ain't That Peculiar," and "I'll Be Doggone."

Gaye's signature Motown album *What's Going On* (1971), a complex mix of jazz and soul infused with social and political commentary, became the soundtrack for a generation. Yet little could have prepared Gaye for the vast commercial success of the 1973 collection of erotic ballads and blues, *Let's Get It On*. After signing with Columbia Records in 1982, the album *Midnight Love*, with its scorching "Sexual Healing," helped cement his status as one of America's greatest crooners. His unforgettable interpretation of "The Star-Spangled Banner" at the 1983 NBA All-Star Game, recently reborn in Nike's 2008 Beijing Olympics advertising campaign, turned out to be his final public appearance. Gaye was inducted into the Rock and Roll Hall of Fame in 1987.

Earl G. Graves, Sr. (b. 1935): Earl Graves is one of the most successful African American entrepreneurs in American history. He attended Morgan State University and received a degree in economics in 1958. From 1965 to 1968, he served as an aide to Senator Robert F. Kennedy and founded the Earl G. Graves Associates management consulting firm.

In 1970, Graves's publishing division debuted *Black Enterprise* magazine, a business publication that describes itself as "the premier business news and investment resource for African Americans." Its readership numbers more than three million. He also co-owns a private-equity fund with Travelers Group, which funds minority businesses. From 1990 to 1998, Graves controlled the Pepsi-Cola bottling franchise in Washington, D.C. In 1997, he authored his definitive manifesto, *How to Succeed in Business Without Being White*, which became a *New York Times* and *Washington Post* bestseller.

His alma mater, Morgan State, honored him by renaming its business school the Earl G. Graves School of Business and Management. Graves has served as a director for Daimler AG, manufacturers of Chrysler and Mercedes, and Aetna Life Insurance Company. In 2002, he was named one of the most influential African Americans in corporate America by *Fortune* magazine.

Alex Haley (1921–1992): Born in Ithaca, New York, and raised in Henning, Tennessee, Alex Haley was a prominent journalist and novelist whose work set a new standard for excellence in American letters. Haley joined the U.S. Coast Guard in 1939, where he spent two decades on active duty. It was in the Coast Guard that Haley discovered his passion for writing, spending the last ten years of his service as a military journalist.

After leaving the service in 1959, Haley began writing articles and features for many of the leading popular magazines. His first interview, appearing in the September 1962 issue of *Playboy* magazine, was with jazz artist Miles Davis. After interviewing Malcolm X for *Playboy* in 1965, he collaborated on *The Autobiography of Malcolm X as told to Alex Haley* (1965), which became an instant bestseller. *Time* magazine later named it "one of the top 10 most important nonfiction works of the 20th century."

Shortly after completing Malcolm's story, he plunged into researching the story of Kunta Kinte, an eighteenth-century slave whom Haley claimed as an ancestor. In 1976, after nearly a decade of research, he released his historical novel *Roots: The Saga of an American Family*. The book garnered special citations from the National Book Awards and the Pulitzer Board, and was translated into a successful hit TV miniseries of the same name in 1977, drawing almost 130 million viewers. In 1979, Haley repeated the formula with *Roots: The Next Generation*, and another television miniseries, *Queen* (1993), based on research into his grandmother's mixed-race heritage.

Fannie Lou Hamer (1917–1977): Born in Ruleville, Mississippi, Fannie Lou Hamer was a heroic grassroots civil rights leader, organizing Blacks throughout the rural South during the bloody Mississippi "Freedom Summer." The youngest of twenty children and the granddaughter of slaves, she was forced to leave school at age twelve to find work to help support her family. While working as a plantation timekeeper, her interest in the civil rights struggle led her to attend meetings of the Regional Council of Negro Leadership, an early civil rights organization.

In 1961, Hamer was sterilized without her consent by a White doctor as part of Mississippi's scheme to reduce the population of poor Blacks. As she traveled throughout the state in the summer of 1962 to rally people to vote, she was notified that she was fired from her plantation job and received threats from the police and the Ku Klux Klan. On another trip into the Farm Belt, outside of Winona, Mississippi, Hamer and members of her group were arrested and brutally beaten. Though she needed more than a month to recover, the ordeal only spurred her on to further action.

In 1964, to protest the all-White presidential delegation sent to the Democratic National Convention, Hamer helped organize the Mississippi Freedom Democratic Party. As its vice-chair, she gave a rousing, nationally televised speech that outlined the case for equal voting rights. Though the MFDP was not seated that year, their actions guaranteed integrated delegations in future national conventions. Hamer went on to represent the Mississippi delegation in the 1968 Democratic Convention. She ran for Congress in 1964 and 1965, and continued to make her presence felt in Mississippi politics throughout her life.

Jimi Hendrix (1942–1970): Many consider Johnny Marshall Hendrix to be the greatest, most innovative guitarist of all time. He continually pushed the electronic envelope by fusing down-home Delta Blues with a wild variety of psychedelic sounds. Born in Seattle, Washington, at the age of fifteen he bought his first acoustic guitar for five dollars and began playing local gigs throughout Washington State.

Hendrix was a high school dropout and a brush with the law left him with a choice between jail and entering the military; he enlisted in the army in 1961. After his discharge, he moved to Clarksville, Tennessee, playing in various bands, before relocating to New York City. Throughout the early 1960s, Hendrix would play with such blues, rock, and soul legends as the Isley Brothers, Little Richard, Sam Cooke, and Ike and Tina Turner.

In 1966, having found little success stateside, Hendrix flew to England. In London, he formed a band, The Jimi

Hendrix Experience, with bassist Noel Redding and drummer Mitch Mitchell. His early British success rested on the hit singles "Hey Joe," "Purple Haze," and "The Wind Cries Mary." Upon returning to the United States and delivering a legendary performance at the 1967 Monterey Pop Festival, Hendrix instantly entered the upper echelon of rock stardom. Hendrix delivered three hit studio albums—*Are You Experienced* (1967), *Axis: Bold as Love* (1967), and *Electric Ladyland* (1968)—as well as the explosive live recording *Band of Gypsys* (1970). He was inducted into the Rock and Roll Hall of Fame in 1992 and the UK Music Hall of Fame in 2005. *Rolling Stone* magazine named Hendrix the best guitarist on their list of "100 Greatest Guitarists of All Time."

Billie Holiday (1915–1959): Born in Philadelphia but raised in Baltimore, Billie Holiday, born Eleanora Fagan, was the greatest jazz vocalist of her day—perhaps ever. Poverty, an unstable home, a single mother, and multiple sexual assaults led Holiday, by 1930, to work in a New York City brothel. According to legend, desperate and almost homeless, she sang the blues at a local club so passionately that she moved the audience to tears, prompting the owner to hire her on the spot. In 1933, talent maven John Hammond discovered her singing at Monette's and signed her on to make her recording debut with Benny Goodman.

By the mid-1930s, Holiday was recording under her own name, with many of the finest jazz musicians of the day, including saxophone great Lester Young, who is credited with bequeathing Holiday the sobriquet "Lady Day." Her vocal stylings are noted for her original, improvisational, and intimate approach to lyrics and tempo. Holiday made political waves with her 1939 performance of the antilynching song "Strange Fruit" and stirred hearts with her trademark songs "Fine and Mellow," "God Bless the Child," "Don't Explain," "Good Morning Heartache," and "Lover Man."

Holiday was felled by drug addiction in the 1940s, which led to several run-ins with the law and loss of her ability to work. Although she toured Europe in 1954, she found little work in America, except for an occasional television appearance and concert performance. Her memoir, *Lady Sings the Blues*, was published in 1956, and she made her final recording in 1959, weeks before her mysterious death.

Langston Hughes (1902–1967): Poet, novelist, essayist, editor, and playwright Langston Hughes was a premier literary influence during the Harlem Renaissance and beyond. Born in Joplin, Missouri, and raised in Kansas, Illinois, Ohio, and Mexico, Hughes was named class poet in middle school. Though he briefly attended Columbia University to study engineering, he left the Ivy League to pursue his love of writing and Black culture. Influenced by the poetry of Walt Whitman, Carl Sandburg, Paul Laurence Dunbar, and Claude McKay, Hughes flourished during the Harlem Renaissance. In 1929, he received his degree from Lincoln University and later became a Guggenheim Fellow (1935) and a Rosenwald Fellow (1940).

An extraordinarily prolific writer, Hughes's gift for sociopolitical commentary was revealed in his piercing analysis "The Negro Artist and the Racial Mountain" (1926). He published numerous poetry collections, including *The Weary Blues* (1926), *The Dream Keeper* (1932), and *The First Book of Jazz* (1955). But his classic and most widely anthologized poem is "The Negro Speaks of Rivers." Plays and musicals penned by Hughes include *Mulatto* (1935), *Simply Heavenly* (1957), and *Jericho–Jim Crow* (1964). His popular humor series based on the Black Everyman character, Jesse B. Semple, was serialized in many Black newspapers. Hughes's life is chronicled in two memoirs, *The Big Sea* (1940) and *I Wonder as I Wander* (1956).

In 1960 Hughes received the NAACP Spingarn Medal, and in 1966 he was honored at the First World Festival of Negro Arts in Dakar, Senegal. Hughes's ashes are interred at the Schomburg Center for Research in Black Culture in Harlem beneath an African cosmogram fittingly titled Rivers.

Zora Neale Hurston (1891–1960): A native of Eatonville, Florida, Zora Neale Hurston was a masterful folkloric novelist and essayist of the Harlem Renaissance, as well as a pioneer in the field of anthropology. Hurston studied at Barnard College in New York City at the height of the Harlem Renaissance. Her interest in anthropology led her to study with the brilliant and revolutionary anthropologist Franz Boas. By the mid-1930s, Hurston's ethnology studies had fueled her literary sensibilities, resulting in numerous awards for her short stories, plays, and novels. However, it was the publication of *Their Eyes Were Watching God* (1937) that has remained her most inspiring and popular work.

During the '40s and '50s, Hurston's views often ran counter to the collectivist sentiments of her contemporaries, perhaps causing an appreciation of her work to be delayed. Yet it is impossible to overstate the significance of Hurston's influence on the development of the African American literary canon, with such works as *Mules and Men* (1935) and the novel *Moses, Man of the Mountain* (1939) standing out as some of the best writing of its day.

Hurston's importance as an African American writer was nearly lost. However, through the efforts of contemporary writers such as Alice Walker, Hurston has become enshrined in America's literary landscape. Today, her contributions are commemorated annually at the Hurston/Wright Foundation Awards and the Zora Neale Hurston Festival of the Arts and Humanities in Eatonville, Florida.

Jesse L. Jackson, Sr. (b. 1941): Born in Greenville, South Carolina, Jesse Jackson came of age during the civil rights era under the wing of Martin Luther King. The young, athletic Jackson was enrolled in a number of colleges before transferring to the Chicago Theological Seminary, but he dropped out in 1966 to commit himself full-time to the struggle for equality. After joining Dr. King's Southern Christian Leadership Conference (SCLC), Jackson rose quickly, successfully taking over Chicago's Operation Breadbasket from 1967 to 1971.

After Dr. King's assassination, Jackson clashed with SCLC officials and in 1971 left to form Operation PUSH (People United to Save Humanity). Throughout the '70s, Jackson developed Operation PUSH's organizational infrastructure, focusing on economic, racial, and social justice issues across America. He later became an international peace envoy, intervening in Syria in 1983 and Cuba in 1984 to win the release of American prisoners. In 1984, Jackson made his first historic bid to be president of the United States. Though he would receive only 21 percent of the primary vote, Jackson's progressive "Rainbow Coalition" paved the way for a new generation of African American politicians in America.

In 1997, Jackson founded the Wall Street Project, an organization committed to providing more business and employment opportunities for minorities. A noted media personality, Jackson hosts the nationally syndicated radio talk show *Keep Hope Alive with Rev. Jesse Jackson*. He was honored with the NAACP Spingarn Medal in 1989 and the Presidential Medal of Freedom in 2000.

Michael Jackson (b. 1958): Michael Jackson has become the most famous performer the world has ever known. He is the seventh child of the famous Jackson family of Gary, Indiana. He debuted on the music scene at age eleven as the impish lead singer of the Jackson Five, singing "I Want You Back" and later "The Love You Save," both of which reached No. 1 on the Billboard Hot 100.

The phenomenal success of the Jackson Five during the Motown years (1968–1975) positioned Jackson as a dynamic performer of memorable ballads. In 1979, composer Quincy Jones transformed Jackson's solo career. While his first record with Jones, *Off the Wall* (1979), would break through many commercial boundaries, it was the follow-up *Thriller* (1982) that launched Michael Jackson to superstardom. With the unstoppable combination of power-pop musical production, spectacular live performances, and an early mastery of the newly created "music video," Jackson was able to cross over into mainstream America as no African American performer had done before or has done since. Later, hit albums such as *Bad* (1987) and *Dangerous* (1991) solidified his position as "The King of Pop."

Jackson's pop career has been exceptional, including winning thirteen Grammy Awards and charting thirteen No. 1 singles. He is also a double inductee in the Rock and Roll Hall of Fame (1997 and 2001).

John H. Johnson (1918–2005): Founder of the largest and most successful African American publishing company in U.S. history, John Johnson had amassed a personal fortune estimated at more than $500 million when he joined the ranks of the Forbes 400 list of wealthiest Americans. Johnson's legendary media and cosmetics empire was rooted in helping African Americans become better informed and more fashionable. Born in Arkansas City, Arkansas, Johnson's family moved to Chicago in the 1930s, where he attended high school and studied at the University of Chicago and Northwestern University. He launched his first magazine, *Negro Digest*, in 1942, which later became *Black World*.

Encouraged by the positive reception for *Negro Digest*, Johnson quickly moved to expand his fledgling publishing company. In August 1945, the first issue of *Ebony* magazine hit the newsstands. One of the first to recognize the purchasing power of the African American community, Johnson Publishing provided Black consumers with fashion, entertainment, and commentary that spoke directly to them. *Ebony*—and later *Jet*, *Black Stars*, and *Ebony Jr.*—broke down socioeconomic barriers and uplifted the race. Johnson also established the Ebony Fashion Fair and Fashion Fair Cosmetics as a community extravaganza that gave Black women the encouragement and opportunity to see themselves as beautiful and cosmopolitan.

In 1993, Johnson Publishing celebrated its fiftieth anniversary, and the founder released a bestselling autobiography, *Succeeding Against the Odds*. The recipient of numerous honors, Johnson was awarded the Presidential Medal of Freedom in 1996.

Quincy Jones (b. 1933): Visionary musician, bandleader, composer, and producer, Quincy Jones helped define the American cultural landscape in the twentieth century through his brilliant work in the worlds of jazz, pop, and cinema. Jones was born in Chicago. His musical career took flight as a child, and as a young man he joined Lionel Hampton's band. Jones played trumpet and arranged charts for Hampton until 1953, then wrote for Tommy Dorsey, Sarah Vaughan, Duke Ellington, and Ray Charles. In 1956, he acted as music director for Dizzy Gillespie's overseas big-band tour.

In 1964, he composed the score for Sidney Lumet's *The Pawnbroker* (1964), the first of over thirty film assignments. Jones's civil rights activism began by supporting the work of Dr. King's Operation Breadbasket, and initiating efforts to help African American artists gain the success and recognition they deserved. He continued to compose and record, creating a string of chart-topping albums and successful film scores, such as *Walking in Space* (1969), *Smackwater Jack* (1971), and *Body Heat* (1974). In 1975, Jones founded Qwest Productions and produced Michael Jackson's *Off the Wall* and *Thriller*, launching the singer into international superstardom.

In 1985, Jones coproduced and scored Steven Spielberg's *The Color Purple*, and conducted and produced the "We Are the World" famine relief benefit recording. In 1993, Jones and David Saltzman formed QDE, which published *Vibe* magazine and produced *The Fresh Prince of Bel-Air*. As the most nominated Grammy artist of all time, Jones has won twenty-six Grammys and an Emmy Award, and has received seven Oscar nominations.

Michael Jordan (b. 1963): Born in Brooklyn and raised in North Carolina, Michael Jordan is considered the greatest basketball player—perhaps the greatest athlete—of all time. Equally important, Jordan, as a brand, forever redefined marketing and advertising in American culture. Though baseball was Jordan's first love, he secured a full basketball scholarship to the University of North Carolina in 1981. He led the Tar Heels to the 1982 NCAA championship and was the College Player of the Year in 1984. The Chicago Bulls drafted him that same year. With his tremendous physical agility, ball-handling skill, and the seemingly magical ability to score at will—not to mention his trademark slam dunks from the free throw line—"Air" Jordan became an instant hit with fans.

Jordan's early years with the Bulls often ended in losing seasons and play-off disappointments. It wasn't until 1991 that Jordan won his first NBA championship series, in what would be the beginning of a brilliant back-to-back-to-back "three-peat." Shocking the world in 1992, Jordan left the NBA to pursue a baseball career. His career in professional baseball fizzled, however, and he rejoined the Bulls in 1995, guiding them to three additional titles from 1996 through 1998.

Honored many times in his illustrious career, Jordan won five Most Valuable Player awards, ten all-NBA first team honors, nine all-defense first honors, fourteen NBA all-star game appearances, and three all-star MVP awards. He earned ten scoring titles, six NBA finals MVP awards, and the 1988 NBA Defensive Player of the Year Award.

Jackie Joyner-Kersee (b. 1962): Jackie Joyner-Kersee was born in East St. Louis, Illinois. Her track-and-field performances have ranked her as one of the greatest Olympic female athletes of all time. Inspired by a 1975 film about all-around female athlete extraordinaire Babe Zaharias, Joyner-Kersee entered the University of California at Los Angeles in 1980, excelling at both track and field and basketball. Her phenomenal athleticism propelled her and her fellow Bruins to four years of winning seasons. In 1998, she was selected as one of the fifteen greatest UCLA women's basketball players of all time, having scored more than one thousand points during her college career.

Ultimately, Joyner-Kersee's ability as a heptathlete and long jumper would bring her international recognition. She holds the world record in the heptathlon and second best in the long jump on the all-time list. She competed in the 1984, 1988, 1992, and 1996 Summer Olympics, as well as the 1986 and 1998 Goodwill Games. She briefly played pro basketball for the Richmond Rage. Joyner-Kersee earned four world championship gold medals, as well as three gold, one silver, and two bronze Olympic medals. *Sports Illustrated* magazine voted her the greatest female athlete of the twentieth century.

Since her retirement, Joyner-Kersee has dedicated herself to improving the quality of life in the East St. Louis community where she was raised. In 1988, she founded the Jackie Joyner-Kersee Foundation, providing resources to those in need. She is also a founding member of Athletes for Hope.

Coretta Scott King (1927–2006): Coretta Scott King is remembered primarily as the extraordinary wife of America's greatest civil rights leader, Dr. Martin Luther King, Jr. However, she herself was a champion for civil rights and a constant advocate for America's neediest citizens before, during, and many years after her life with Dr. King.

Raised in Alabama, Coretta Scott pursued her passion for music at the New England Conservatory of Music in

Boston, where she met and married Martin in 1953. After they graduated, the Kings relocated to Montgomery, Alabama, where Pastor King set up his ministry at Dexter Avenue Baptist Church. In 1955, the young minister led the Montgomery Bus Boycott, and together the Kings were thrust into the forefront of the early civil rights movement.

Throughout the civil rights campaigns, Scott King supported her husband by being at his side and organizing Freedom Concerts on the protest trail. An activist in her own right, Scott King joined the Women's Strike for Peace in 1961 and was a delegate to the 1962 Disarmament Conference in Geneva. On April 4, 1968, her husband was murdered in Memphis. Shortly after that, Scott King began work in Atlanta to establish the Martin Luther King Jr. Center for Nonviolent Social Change, which opened its doors to the public in 1981. She served as CEO of the center and, in 1986, after enormous effort, her seventeen-year-long campaign for a national holiday honoring her husband succeeded. Coretta Scott King remained active in the fight against racial and economic injustice until her death in 2006.

Martin Luther King, Jr. (1929–1968):

Born in Atlanta, Dr. King became the face and voice of the twentieth-century nonviolent civil rights struggle, which aimed to hold America true to its democratic promise. An activist, scholar, orator, and dedicated theologian, Dr. King came to represent American greatness and sacrifice as the United States struggled to transcend its history of devastating racial oppression.

The descendant of a long line of Baptist ministers, King earned his doctorate in theology at Boston University in 1955. He met his future wife, Coretta Scott, while studying in Boston, and the two were wed in 1953. He then accepted the pastorate at Dexter Avenue Baptist Church in Montgomery, Alabama. In 1956, he emerged as the leader of the Montgomery Bus Boycott. The success of the boycott thrust Dr. King onto the national stage. This unprecedented triumph led King and other southern Black ministers to establish the Southern Christian Leadership Conference (SCLC) in 1957. The SCLC provided Dr. King with the necessary infrastructure and resources to mount large-scale civil rights campaigns.

In 1963, during the historic March on Washington, King gave voice to the American civil rights movement in his "I Have a Dream" speech. Later that year, he was named Man of the Year by *Time* magazine. In 1964 he was awarded the Nobel Peace Prize. On April 4, 1968, King was assassinated in Memphis on the balcony of the Lorraine Motel. Nearly a decade later, he was posthumously awarded the Presidential Medal of Freedom. In 1986, Congress declared the third Monday of January Martin Luther King, Jr. Day.

Jacob Lawrence (1917–2000):

One of the most prominent African American artists of the twentieth century, Jacob Lawrence was raised in Atlantic City, New Jersey, and moved to New York City when he was thirteen. Demonstrating an early artistic aptitude, Lawrence studied with artist Charles H. Alston at the Harlem Art Workshop in 1932. By the time he was twenty-one, Lawrence's talent was on display at the Baltimore Museum of Art. However, it was his *Migration of the Negro* series—a masterful set of sixty expressionist paintings that told the story of the Great Migration of African Americans from the rural South to the urban North after World War I—that brought him international recognition.

During World War II, Lawrence served in the Coast Guard. After his discharge, he received a Guggenheim Fellowship, which allowed him to rededicate himself to painting. During this period, Lawrence returned to historical themes, and his colorful and energetic work gained wide recognition in shows at mainstream American museums.

Lawrence taught at several universities, including Black Mountain College, Pratt Institute, and the University of Washington. Revered as one of the greatest twentieth-century American painters, his painting *The Builders* now hangs in the White House. Lawrence received a National Institute of Arts and Letters Award in 1953 and the NAACP Spingarn Medal in 1970. He was elected to the American Academy of Arts and Letters in 1983.

Malcolm X (El-Hajj Malik El-Shabazz) (1925–1965):

Born in Omaha, Nebraska, Malcolm Little's transformation from street thug to controversial spokesman of the Nation of Islam to national symbol of Black pride and self-empowerment is one of the pivotal stories of the 1960s civil rights era. Following the loss of both parents, Little went through a series of foster homes and later entered a world of crime in Boston and New York City. In 1945, at the age of twenty, he was sentenced to eight to ten years in prison for burglary.

While in prison, Malcolm Little converted to Islam and changed his name to Malcolm X. Upon his parole in 1952, Malcolm X joined the Nation of Islam under the leadership of the Honorable Elijah Muhammad and he quickly ascended in the organization. By 1954, he was the head of the Nation's Temple No. 7 in Harlem. For more than a decade, Malcolm X was the passionate and outspoken voice of the Nation of Islam, and his profile as a Black leader rose exponentially. His relationship with the Nation soured over time and in March 1964 Malcolm X left the Nation of Islam.

Malcolm X's 1964 visit to Mecca proved to be a turning point in his spiritual and intellectual development. After returning to America, he reestablished himself as a major Black leader under his new name, El-Hajj Malik El-Shabazz.

In 1965, he wrote *The Autobiography of Malcolm X as told to Alex Haley*, named in 1999 by *Time* magazine as one of the "Top 10 nonfiction works of the 20th century." On February 21, 1965, Malcolm X was assassinated while delivering a speech at the Audubon Ballroom in Harlem.

Thurgood Marshall (1908–1993): Leading the charge to end America's shameful, entrenched segregation policies, Thurgood Marshall broke through the legal and judiciary's color line by becoming the first African American to serve on the Supreme Court. A Baltimore native, Marshall graduated from high school in 1925 and enrolled at Lincoln University, where his fellow students included writer Langston Hughes and future Ghanaian president Kwame Nkrumah. Marshall applied to the University of Maryland Law School in 1930, only to be denied due to the school's segregationist policy. That same year, Marshall was accepted at the Howard University School of Law.

After setting up a private practice in Baltimore—and helping to overturn the University of Maryland's racist segregation policies—Marshall followed his Howard University mentor, Charles Hamilton Houston, to New York City and joined the legal team of the NAACP. In 1940, at the age of thirty-two, Marshall was appointed chief counsel for the NAACP. Marshall won twenty-nine of the thirty-two cases he argued before the Supreme Court from 1940 to 1961. His landmark case was the 1954 *Brown v. Board of Education of Topeka, Kansas*, which overturned the legal basis for segregation in America. In 1961, President John F. Kennedy appointed him to the Second Circuit Court of Appeals.

While serving as a circuit judge, he ruled on 112 cases, all of them upheld by the Supreme Court from 1961 to 1965. President Lyndon Johnson named him U.S. solicitor general in 1965 and appointed him to the Supreme Court in 1967, where he became a standard-bearer for constitutional protection of individual rights.

Thelonious Monk (1917–1982): One of jazz's unique personalities, and often regarded as its greatest creative genius, Thelonious Monk, through his work in the bebop idiom, helped define American music for a generation. He began playing piano at age nine and progressed with virtually no formal training. After leaving high school, Monk toured briefly with an evangelical preacher before joining the house band at Minton's Playhouse in 1940.

The bebop genre was born in Minton's with the combined talents of innovators such as Charlie Parker, Dizzy Gillespie, Max Roach, Kenny Clarke, Miles Davis, and Monk. In 1944, Monk recorded his first session with saxophone great Coleman Hawkins, and made his first recordings as a band leader for Blue Note in 1947. After having his New York City cabaret card revoked due to legal problems, he was not allowed to perform in New York City clubs for much of the 1950s. Despite these restrictions, Monk continued to compose and record. His idiosyncratic playing—at times seemingly random and offbeat to the untrained and unappreciative ear—often frustrated critics and musicians. Yet Monk's playing revolutionized modern jazz sensibilities.

On the Riverside label in the late 1950s and the Columbia label in the 1960s, Monk recorded some of his most important work, such as *Brilliant Corners* (1956), *Solo Monk* (1964), *Straight, No Chaser* (1966), *Underground* (1967), and *Thelonious Monk with John Coltrane* (1957). In 1964, Monk appeared on the cover of *Time* magazine. He made his final tour in 1971. In 1993, he was posthumously awarded the Grammy Lifetime Achievement Award.

Toni Morrison (b. 1931): Born Chloe Anthony Wofford in Lorain, Ohio, Nobel laureate Toni Morrison has become one of America's leading literary voices. Her novel *Beloved* is considered among the greatest American novels ever written. The second of four children, the young Morrison expressed remarkable interest in books and literature, devouring works by such literary greats as Jane Austen, Gustave Flaubert, and Leo Tolstoy. In 1949, she entered Howard University and later attended Cornell University for graduate studies. She returned to Howard to teach English in 1957. In 1964, she began work as an editor for Random House. It was there that she started writing her first novel, *The Bluest Eye* (1970).

Other books followed, among them: *Sula* (1974), which was nominated for a National Book Award; *Song of Solomon* (1977), which won the National Book Critics Circle Award; and her magnum opus, *Beloved* (1987), which won the Pulitzer Prize for Fiction. Her nonfiction works, including *The Black Book* (1974) and *Playing in the Dark: Whiteness and the Literary Imagination* (1992), have also received critical acclaim.

In 1980, President Jimmy Carter appointed Morrison to the National Council on the Arts. In 1983, she left her job at Random House after almost twenty years. In 1986, she wrote a play, *Dreaming Emmett*, and the libretto for the opera *Margaret Garner*. In 1987, Princeton University named Toni Morrison to the Robert F. Goheen Chair in the Humanities.

Motown (founded in 1959): From a small, two-story house in Detroit called "Hitsville USA" former car-assembly-line worker and songwriter Berry Gordy, Jr., would help create an urban sound that resonated with African Americans while also appealing to White listeners, reshaping American popular culture forever. In 1959, Gordy borrowed eight hundred dollars from his family to start his own recording company. Less than a year later, Motown was born.

A brilliant pool of talented and inspired musicians, songwriters, and producers turned Motown into the "hit factory" that made Smokey Robinson and the Miracles, Marvin Gaye, Diana Ross and the Supremes, the Four Tops, the Temptations, and the Jackson Five into household names. Desiring full creative control, Gordy was intimately involved in the writing and recording process, approving every track before its inclusion on an album. Between 1964 and 1967, Motown scored fourteen No. 1 pop singles. In 1966, no less than 75 percent of Motown's releases found their way onto the charts.

But it was the Motown Sound that was truly a marvel: irresistibly danceable, with melodic guitar lines, popping chord changes, and soulful gospel vocal inflections supported by rich string sections and tight horn arrangements. The legacy of Motown is undeniably embedded in the sound of American popular music. Gordy moved Motown from Detroit to Los Angeles in 1972. He eventually sold the label to MCA Records in 1988 for $61 million. The Hitsville USA house in Detroit survives as an active museum honoring Motown's contribution to world culture.

NAACP (founded in 1909): One of America's oldest, most respected, and most influential civil rights organizations, the National Association for the Advancement of Colored People (NAACP) has led the fight to make America a safer, more secure, and more prosperous country for all of its citizens. Born out of post-Reconstruction disillusionment and Jim and Jane Crow's viciousness, the NAACP brought together a cross-cultural and multi-racial coalition, aiming to "revive the spirit of the abolitionists" in twentieth-century America.

Founded by such notable crusaders as W. E. B. Du Bois, Ida B. Wells, Archibald Grimké, and Henry Moskowitz, the NAACP led early fights for racial equality in the courts and in the streets. From protesting the racist propaganda film *Birth of a Nation* to publicizing in major newspapers the shameful reality of race-based lynchings, the NAACP took principled stances against disenfranchisement and Jim Crow laws, while delivering concrete results throughout the 1900s.

As the postwar generation reentered American life, the NAACP, through the dedicated leadership of Roy Wilkins, kept pace, often becoming the direct target for violence: NAACP attorney Arthur Shores's house was bombed and Field Director Medgar Evers was murdered in 1963. The organization's desegregation efforts—including nonviolent sit-ins, voter registration and empowerment, and school integration—helped provide the foundation for the civil rights movement's success. Over the years, the NAACP attracted new leaders like Benjamin Hooks, Myrlie Evers-Williams and Julian Bond, even as it faced pointed questions about its relevance and criticism from activist organizations. The NAACP's efforts remain as relevant today as they were in 1909.

Barack Obama (b. 1961): Illinois senator Barack Obama rose from near obscurity to become the first African American to earn his party's nomination for president of the United States. Born in Hawaii to a White mother from Kansas and a Black father from Kenya, Obama graduated from Columbia University in New York in 1983, before moving to Illinois to work as a community organizer advocating for poor families on Chicago's South Side. In 1988, Obama left to study at Harvard University Law School, becoming the first African American to head the prestigious *Harvard Law Review*.

After Harvard, Obama returned to Chicago to teach constitutional law at the University of Chicago Law School. From 1996 to 2004, Obama served in the Illinois State Senate. He ran for the U.S. Senate in 2004, winning with nearly 70 percent of the vote. In Congress, Obama forged bipartisan relationships to reduce weapons worldwide and provide transparency in government spending.

His speech during the 2004 Democratic National Convention launched the junior senator into the national spotlight. On February 10, 2007, Senator Obama announced his candidacy for president of the United States. His innovative and inspiring campaign harnessed the strength and energy of voters unseen in American politics for decades. The result was unprecedented fund-raising and record voter turnout. In his historic speech on race, Obama provided a twenty-first-century entry point for a frank discussion on how far we've come and how far we have to go. After a long and, at times, fierce primary battle Senator Obama captured the 2008 Democratic nomination.

Charlie Parker (1920–1955): Born in Kansas City, Kansas, saxophonist Charlie "Bird" Parker injected an unprecedented depth and intelligence into jazz through his innovative harmony, melody, and rhythm. On par with celebrated musicians Louis Armstrong and Duke Ellington, Parker's development of the bebop idiom helped push jazz to new heights.

Parker began playing the alto saxophone at age thirteen. Lacking formal training, he was supposedly tossed out of his high school band. However, he persisted, reportedly practicing fifteen hours a day. In 1939, Parker relocated to New York City and joined pianist Jay McShann's band in 1940. A year later, he was playing with pianist Earl "Fatha" Hines's band when he met fellow band member Dizzy Gillespie. The duo later teamed up with luminaries such as pianist Thelonious Monk, guitarist Charlie Christian, and drummer Max Roach—among many others—for after-hours sessions at Monroe's Uptown House and Minton's Playhouse in Harlem. These artists—led by Parker's revolutionary musical approach and an urge to create a deeply Africanized version of jazz—gave birth to one of the greatest musical movements in American history: bebop.

Some of the best examples of Parker's alto sax mastery can be heard on recordings such as *The Charlie Parker Story* (1945), *Diz 'n Bird at Carnegie Hall* (1947), *Bird on 52nd Street* (1948), and the classic *Jazz at Massey Hall* (1953). Despite his short-lived career, Parker's impressive body of recordings has continued to influence jazz, setting the bar high for decades of musicians to come.

Gordon Parks (1912–2006): Gordon Parks, born in Fort Scott, Kansas, was a true Renaissance artist. He was an accomplished photographer, film director, writer, and composer. His iconic work highlighted the daily realities of African Americans, capturing the broad range of rich individual stories through the lens of his camera and the keys of his typewriter.

Parks was the youngest of fifteen children, and at age fifteen, after his mother's death, he struck out on his own, working odd jobs to support himself. Inspired by images of migrant workers in a magazine, Parks bought his first camera from a pawnshop. His natural talent would make him a sought-after photographer and photojournalist. He was the first African American to shoot for *Vogue* magazine in 1944 and the first African American photographer at *Life* magazine in 1948, where he would remain until 1972. Parks chronicled many of the top news headlines and celebrated personalities in the latter half of the twentieth century.

In 1971, Parks put his cinematic talents on full display. His leather-clad, no-nonsense detective hero, *Shaft* (1971), ushered in a new film genre and rewrote the rules for Black popular entertainment. Parks was equally able to display the same great versatility behind the movie camera as he did behind the still camera, in such works as the semi-autobiographical *The Learning Tree* (1963) and *Leadbelly* (1976). His outstanding work in photography and film has been widely acclaimed and exhibited in museums, private collections, and cinema archives.

Rosa Parks (1913–2005): Born in Tuskegee, Alabama, Rosa Louise Parks (née McCauley) became a legendary symbol of the civil rights movement for her courageous refusal to give up her bus seat to a White man. Far beyond her single inspiring example, Parks represented the power of collective strength in social and political organizing. Growing up in the Jim Crow South, Parks's life was shaped by the racist apartheid entrenched all around her. Stresses forced her to drop out of school at a young age. Nevertheless, she finished her high school education in 1933 and went on to attend Alabama State Teachers College.

Parks's participation in the civil rights movement began in the 1930s. By 1943, she had become secretary of the local NAACP branch. In 1955, at the behest of liberal White patrons, Parks attended a pivotal civil rights leadership training workshop at Highlander Folk School in Tennessee. By 1955, the NAACP was working vigorously, locally and nationally, to challenge and overturn bus segregation. In quiet, respectable Rosa Parks, organizers found exactly what they needed. On December 1, 1955, Parks's refusal to give up her bus seat to Whites evolved into a full-blown movement. Her arrest led to the successful 381-day Montgomery Bus Boycott, led by a young Martin Luther King.

Throughout her life Parks remained an integral part of the civil rights movement. In 1965, she went to work for Congressman John Conyers, where she remained until her retirement in 1988. She was awarded the Presidential Medal of Freedom in 1996 and the Congressional Medal of Honor in 1999.

Sidney Poitier (b. 1927): Born in Miami, Florida, but raised in the Bahamas, Sidney Poitier's brilliant and dignified film performances challenged bigoted stereotypes, bringing issues of race and inequity into the popular consciousness of America. After his service in the army, Poitier decided to try his hand at acting, debuting on Broadway in an all-Black version of the Greek play *Lysistrata*. His career continued to progress and he made his screen debut in *No Way Out* (1950), receiving critical praise. While many opportunities were not offered to African American actors of the day, Poitier won significant roles in *Cry, the Beloved Country* (1951), *Blackboard Jungle* (1955), and *The Defiant Ones* (1958), for which he received an Academy Award nomination.

Poitier returned to the stage in 1959 to star in Lorraine Hansberry's *A Raisin in the Sun*. His performance as Walter Lee Younger earned him a Tony Award nomination for Best Actor. He reprised that role for the film version in 1961. Poitier's early success culminated with his Academy Award for Best Actor—the first for an African American male—for his starring role in *Lilies of the Field* (1963). Poitier continued to deliver classic performances in *A Patch of Blue* (1965), *In the Heat of the Night* (1967), *Guess Who's Coming to Dinner* (1967), and *To Sir, with Love* (1967). Among the awards for Poitier's outstanding work are the Kennedy Center Honors (1995), Screen Actors Guild (SAG) Life Achievement Award (1999), and the NAACP Image Award Hall of Fame (2000).

Adam Clayton Powell, Jr. (1908–1972): Born in New Haven, Connecticut, congressman and minister Adam Clayton Powell, Jr., blazed political trails like none before or since, earning him the respect and admiration of a generation. Powell was the son of prominent Abyssinian Baptist Church minister Adam Clayton Powell, Sr. Earning his master's in religious education from Columbia University in 1932, Powell succeeded his father as pastor of the legendary Harlem church in 1937.

During the Depression, Powell became a well-known community activist, fighting for housing rights, employment, and education equity. In 1941, Powell became the first African American elected to the New York City Council, thanks in part to a progressive electoral system known as proportional representation.

Three years later, Powell was elected to represent New York's Twenty-second District in the United States Congress. He was New York's first African American congressman, and one of the first African Americans to be elected to Congress since the end of Reconstruction. Powell often clashed with his party's more racist tendencies during his nearly twenty-six uninterrupted years in office, breaking ranks over civil rights to support Eisenhower in 1956. As chair of the Education and Labor Committee, Powell helped push through increases in the minimum wage, vocational education standards, and stronger labor protection laws. He was a major supporter of President Kennedy's New Frontier and President Johnson's Great Society social and economic uplift programs.

Prince (b. 1958): Born in Minneapolis, Prince Rogers Nelson exploded onto the music scene in the 1980s and has continued to challenge, dazzle, and innovate ever since. Hailing from a family of musicians, Prince was named after his father's jazz band, and by age fourteen, the self-taught multi-instrumentalist was performing regularly. At eighteen, Prince had crafted enough impressive solo material to secure a lucrative recording contract with Warner Bros.

From 1980 to 1984, Prince produced, recorded, and performed all the material for four full-length albums. Combining his signature mix of funk, pop, rock, and sex, he electrified fans and stupefied critics with eclectic, risqué stage performances that crossed social and sexual boundaries. His breakthrough record *1999* (1982) ushered Prince into his permanent reign in American popular culture. By creating music that cut across different styles and demographics, he was able to find success in ways that hadn't been seen in a generation.

With the release of the film and album versions of *Purple Rain* (1984), Prince became a household name. Grossing more than $80 million at the box office, *Purple Rain* yielded five hit singles, an Oscar for Best Original Sound Score, and two Grammys. Prince has gone on to produce more than two dozen records and has earned numerous awards and consistent praise, despite legal battles with Warner Bros. that resulted in his famous "Artist Formally Known As" name change. In 2007, Prince performed an unforgettable halftime show during Super Bowl XLI, showing no sign—or intention—of slowing down his creative genius.

Richard Pryor (1940–2005): Born in Peoria, Illinois, Richard Pryor became one of America's seminal comedians through his irreverent, insightful, and no-holds-barred humor. After a brief stint in the army, Pryor made his way to New York City in 1963 to follow in the footsteps of Bill Cosby, his forerunner. Pryor soon gained notoriety as a stand-up comedian, opening for musical acts such as Bob Dylan, Richie Havens, and Nina Simone. Television performances on *The Ed Sullivan Show* and *The Tonight Show* thrust Pryor into the national spotlight, and he began performing regularly on the A-list circuit. In 1969, Pryor made his way to the epicenter of the turbulent '60s, Berkeley, California, where he would begin honing his explosive yet poignant style. Pryor's raw stage act and recorded albums exposed the underbelly of American racism while introducing mainstream audiences to the many facets of African American life.

Through the '70s and '80s, Pryor's talent contributed to numerous bestselling films, including *Silver Streak* (1976), *Stir Crazy* (1980), *The Toy* (1982), and *Brewster's Millions* (1985). He regularly released live albums—including *That Nigger's Crazy* (1974), *. . . Is It Something I Said?* (1975), and *Bicentennial Nigger* (1976). He was also a recognized comedic writer, working on such projects as the movie *Blazing Saddles* (1974) and the television show *Sanford and Son* (1972–1977). Pryor won five Grammy Awards for his recordings and the American Comedy Award's Lifetime Achievement Honor. He was the first recipient of the Mark Twain Prize for American Humor (1998).

Paul Robeson (1898–1976): Superb athlete, gifted thespian, uncompromised humanitarian—Paul Robeson exemplified African American genius in the early twentieth century. Born in Princeton, New Jersey, he attended Rutgers University as a star scholar and athlete, earning his keep through singing and dramatic performances. In 1923, he graduated from Columbia University with a degree in law.

Robeson's early recognition came from his performances on the stage and screen. With his dashing good looks and tremendous bass singing voice, Robeson starred in numerous stage productions, including his now-famous lead role in the 1930 London staging of *Othello*. Throughout the mid-1920s and into the 1940s, Robeson appeared in eleven films, including the much-praised *Show Boat* (1936), despite the widespread racism he encountered in American productions.

Robeson was a fervent champion of civil rights his entire life, speaking out early and often against murderous lynchings in the United States. He traveled across the world in defense of justice—from striking mining camps in Wales and antifascist Spain during their civil war, to the campaign trails of progressive U.S. politicians and before West African leaders—using his position as a cultural icon to infuse legitimacy and hope into noble causes. After the start of the cold war, Robeson was persecuted by the U.S. government for his political leanings, and he suffered, as did many others, for being associated with Socialist or Communist activities. Despite these difficulties, Robeson remained a sought-after talent internationally, and he was revered as a true freedom fighter for human rights and dignity the world over.

Jackie Robinson (1919–1972): Born in Cairo, Georgia, and raised in Pasadena, California, Jackie Robinson became an international symbol of grace, dignity, and triumph after breaking baseball's color barrier in 1947. As a child, Robinson excelled at virtually every sport he tried, eventually becoming a sports legend at the University of California at Los Angeles.

He joined the army in 1942. After his discharge in 1945, Robinson joined the Negro League's Kansas City Monarchs. His phenomenal .387 batting average with the Monarchs attracted the attention of Branch Rickey, president and manager of the Brooklyn Dodgers. After playing for the Dodgers farm team for a year, Robinson made his major league debut on April 15, 1947. Robinson faced constant discrimination, both from opposing teams and from their fans, and often from fellow Dodgers. Yet Dodger management came to his defense and outside hostility eventually united Robinson and his teammates.

In his rookie year, Robinson played 151 games, batted .292, led the National League in stolen bases, and took home the inaugural Rookie of the Year Award. He went on to be selected to the all-star team six times, won National League Most Valuable Player in 1949, and helped the Dodgers win the 1955 World Series. Robinson was inducted into the Baseball Hall of Fame in 1962. His uniform number 42 was retired from all of major league baseball in 1997. Beyond his baseball fame, Robinson worked throughout his life to advance civil rights, receiving the NAACP Spingarn Medal in 1956, as well as serving on their board until 1967.

Tupac Shakur (1971–1996): Tupac Shakur is considered by many to be the most influential rapper of all time. He was born in East Harlem. By the time of his death in 1996, Shakur had risen to international stardom as a gifted lyricist and actor, injecting social and political consciousness into gangsta rap. His mother, Afeni Shakur, was an active member of the Black Panther Party who raised her young son with deep racial pride.

As a teenager, Shakur displayed a gift for performance, starring in local plays and attending the Baltimore School for the Arts. In 1988, Shakur's family moved to Marin City, California. There, among the rappers and DJs, young Tupac discovered his true creative calling. His first entrée into the emerging world of "West Coast" rap came with the single "Same Song." After serving eleven months in jail, Shakur was bailed out by Death Row CEO Suge Knight and produced the double album *All Eyez On Me* (1996). This record exposed the raw nerve of race long ignored by mainstream America. The controversy surrounding the record helped catapult Shakur to instant fame, making him an icon in the African American community and a respected antihero in White suburbs.

Hit records and film appearances followed, making Shakur the bestselling hip-hop artist in the world. Even his violent death did not stop the flow of hits. Shakur's projected image—intentional and calculated—forced America, at the turn of the twenty-first century, to face the righteous rage of a generation of African Americans told to accept the mainstream's convenient deferment of the political and social equality that previous generations had fought so hard to achieve.

Nina Simone (1933–2003): Born in Tryon, North Carolina, Nina Simone possessed unrivaled musical ability as a singer, composer, and pianist. Known as "the High Priestess of Soul," Simone's genre-defying artistry provided the civil rights generation with a crucial touchstone.

Even as a child, Simone displayed prodigious talent, learning to play piano at the age of three. Her abilities earned her a place at The Juilliard School of Music in New York City at age seventeen. In 1958, after playing small clubs and bars for a number of years, Simone got her first big break with the release of her rendition of Gershwin's "I Loves You Porgy," which broke into the Billboard Top 40 (her first and only Top 40 hit in the United States), and her first album, *Little Girl Blue*. By 1964, Simone had become a rising star, surrounding herself with like-minded artists who were using their talents to decry American racism. Simone addressed this head-on in songs such as "Mississippi Goddam," "Strange Fruit," "Four Women," and "To Be Young, Gifted and Black." Her tireless work for the movement—fund-raising, performing at civil rights rallies, and participating in civil rights protests—earned her an additional accolade: "Singer of the Black Revolution."

In 1970, Simone left the United States permanently. Yet her legacy lives on through generations of musicians. Artists—from Aretha Franklin and David Bowie to Timbaland and Lil' Wayne—have covered Simone's work, while many others, in every creative field, have credited her as an influence.

Tommie Smith (b. 1944): Born in Clarksville, Texas, Tommie Smith's iconic Black Power salute during the 1968 Olympic Games' medal ceremony launched him and fellow American John Carlos into the international spotlight and decades of controversy.

Smith's lightning speed was evident in high school, where he began his record-breaking career. After arriving at San Jose State, he excelled in the 100-, 200-, and 400-meter sprints. Smith broke seven individual world records and was a member of several world-record relay teams. In 1968, Smith completed back-to-back Amateur Athletic Union (AAU) 220-meter wins, qualifying him for the Olympic Games. The previous year, Smith—along with co-Olympian Carlos and San Jose State professor Harry Edwards—had founded the Olympic Project for Human Rights. Failing to convince African American athletes to boycott the 1968 Olympics in protest of American and South African apartheid, Smith and Carlos traveled to Mexico City, ready to make a statement.

At the Mexico City Games, Smith won the Gold Medal in the 200-meter dash, setting a new world record of 19.83 seconds. His teammate John Carlos earned the bronze. During the medal ceremonies, supported by Australian silver medalist Peter Norman, Smith and Carlos both raised their gloved, clenched fists in salute as "The Star-Spangled Banner" played throughout the stadium. Their singular act became one of the unforgettable moments in the civil rights era. Smith went on to play pro football briefly before becoming a coach, educator, and lifelong activist. In 1978, he was inducted into the National Track & Field Hall of Fame.

Sarah Vaughan (1924–1980): Born in Newark, New Jersey, Sarah Vaughan brought her multi-octave voice, creativity, artistry, and spontaneity to the world of jazz, influencing generations of singers and musicians. In 1943, the shy, unpolished Vaughan stepped onto the stage in Harlem's famed Apollo Theatre, winning an amateur night competition and officially beginning her musical career.

Shortly after her Apollo debut, Vaughan was hired by famed pianist and band leader Earl "Fatha" Hines to perform as his lead female vocalist alongside renowned baritone Billy Eckstine, trumpeter Dizzy Gillespie, and saxophonist Charlie Parker. By 1945, Vaughan had struck out on a solo career, performing at nightclubs throughout New York City. Recording opportunities soon followed. On the rise as a "bop" star and innovator, her renditions of "Tenderly," "It's Magic," and "Nature Boy" landed her on the hit charts in the late '40s.

It was her shift in the late '40s and early '50s from bop to pop that provided Vaughan with her biggest commercial success. By 1959, her newfound fame peaked with her first gold record, *Broken-Hearted Melody*. Throughout the '70s, Vaughan toured and recorded with the world's jazz and pop luminaries. Though not as widely renowned as some of her female vocal contemporaries, Vaughan's voice is regarded as the best of her generation. An undying influence on

American popular culture, she received *Esquire* magazine's New Star Award in 1947, a 1981 Emmy for Individual Achievement, and numerous Grammys, as well as a star on the Hollywood Walk of Fame.

Alice Walker (b. 1944): Writer, scholar, historian, and activist, Alice Walker has written award-winning fiction that made her the voice for a generation of women and African Americans, linking the struggles of the past with hope for the future. Born the youngest of eight children to sharecropping parents in Eatonton, Georgia, Walker has a fierce intelligence and determination that earned her a full scholarship to Spelman College in Atlanta. Though she ultimately finished her undergraduate work at Sarah Lawrence College in New York, Walker's commitment to the civil rights struggle began at Spelman.

Shortly after college, Walker—who had married and moved to Mississippi—began her writing career, publishing her first book of poems, *Once* (1968), and her first novel, *The Third Life of Grange Copeland* (1970), while continuing her activist work, teaching, and raising her newborn daughter. During this time, Walker also became a leading voice in the feminist movement. Recognizing the triple threat of racism, classism, and sexism faced by women of color in a movement dominated by middle-class Whites, Walker branded her newfound political consciousness "womanism."

Walker's continued dedication to writing throughout the late '70s and early '80s produced three more books of poetry and two novels, the second of which, *The Color Purple* (1982), solidified Walker's towering presence in literature. Walker eventually won both the National Book Award and the Pulitzer Prize for Fiction. *The Color Purple*'s story of triumph in the face of profound racism and sexism became a major cultural and commercial success and was eventually adapted for both the screen and the Broadway stage.

Serena Williams (b. 1981): Serena Williams—currently ranked No. 1 in women's tennis—is the most recent player, of either sex, to hold all four Grand Slam titles at the same time. Tenacious and powerful, Williams spent her early years on the courts of Compton, Califonia. Her style is total domination, and she plays with ruthless efficiency, using a serve that is considered one of the best, if not the best, in all of women's tennis.

Serena won her first tournament when she was four years old. The Williams family moved to Palm Beach Gardens, Florida, in 1991, where Serena quickly followed in her sister's footsteps as a tennis prodigy, going pro in 1995. Two years later she shocked the tennis world when, ranked 304th, she went on to upset top-ranked players Monica Seles and Mary Pierce, eventually finishing the year ranked 99th. In 1998, Serena joined her sister Venus to form a nearly unstoppable doubles team that would sweep the mixed doubles Grand Slam that year.

At the beginning of the new millennium, Serena has elevated her game to superstar status, winning three out of the four Grand Slam titles in 2002, almost three dozen total titles at the time of this writing, and doubles gold medals with her sister in the Sydney and, most recently, Beijing Olympics.

Venus Williams (b. 1980): Venus Williams is one of tennis's most dynamic and successful superstars. She displays an aggressive, quick game never before seen on the women's court. Venus started playing tennis before the age of five in Compton, California. In 1991, the Williams family moved to Palm Beach Gardens, Florida, where Venus would rapidly emerge as one of tennis's most promising stars.

Venus played her first professional match in 1994 at the age of fourteen. By 1997, she was ranked twenty-fifth in the world, making her Grand Slam debut at the French Open. It was the first time an unseeded woman player had reached the tournament's final and the first time an African American woman had been in the final since 1957. With her long reach, skillful volleys, and powerful serve, Williams won her first Women's Tennis Association singles championship in 1998. Two years later, in 2000, she won her first Grand Slam singles title, defeating top-ranked women's player Martina Hingis, her sister Serena, and the defending champion, Lindsay Davenport, at Wimbledon. At the U.S. Open that same year, Venus defeated Hingis and Davenport again. At the Sydney Olympic Games, she won the singles gold medal. In 2002, Venus became the No. 1 ranked woman in the world. That same year, she and her sister Serena won their second doubles title at Wimbledon.

August Wilson (1945–2005): Born in Pittsburgh, August Wilson, the son of a German immigrant father and an African American mother, rose from unassuming beginnings to provide American theater with some of its finest late-century pieces. Wilson's mixed-race family faced much of the direct discrimination of the day, and he dropped out of high school at fifteen. Yet in his dedication to self-education—he used the Pittsburgh Carnegie Library so often it eventually provided him a degree in place of his diploma—we see the curious, committed, inspired Wilson who would rise to become a famed man of letters.

After a short stint in the army, Wilson dedicated himself to writing. In 1965, his first effort, *Recycled*, was performed in small and often obscure community theaters. In 1976, he helped found the Kuntu Writers Workshop, which aimed "to develop and celebrate Black writers and enhance cultural enrichment in the global community." Beginning in the early 1980s and continuing through his death in 2005, Wilson began producing his groundbreaking opus, the Pittsburgh Cycle—ten plays, each set in a different twentieth-century decade, all focused on portraying African American life in the Hill District of Pittsburgh. As one critic noted, the Pittsburgh Cycle is unprecedented in its "concept, size, and cohesion." Two of the plays—*Fences* (1985) and *The Piano Lesson* (1989)—won Pulitzer Prizes for Drama. A litany of other awards followed for Wilson. Broadway's Virginia Theatre was renamed the August Wilson Theatre in his honor.

Oprah Winfrey (b. 1954): Born in Kosciusko, Mississippi, Oprah Winfrey has become one of the most famous, well-respected, and influential women in America. Her rise to international superstardom has made her a brand unto herself and the first African American woman to be a billionaire.

Winfrey started her broadcasting career at age seventeen as a part-time news broadcaster for WVOL Radio in Nashville. After graduating from Tennessee State University, Winfrey moved to Baltimore, where she found her knack for the talk show format, cohosting a local show, *People Are Talking*, in 1978. In 1983, Winfrey relocated to Chicago and began hosting a low-rated half-hour local morning talk show, *AM Chicago*. Within a year she had transformed her time slot into a ratings machine, extending it to an hour, and in September 1985 renamed it *The Oprah Winfrey Show*. In 1987, Winfrey claimed the No. 1 nationally syndicated talk show on television, earning three Daytime Emmy Awards. During this time, Winfrey also found time to act, earning an Academy Award nomination for her role in *The Color Purple* (1985).

The consummate communications mogul, Winfrey built a media empire rooted in her innovative production company, Harpo Productions, Inc. From that base she has become a successful film producer, book advocate, magazine publisher, subscription radio entrepreneur, and the co-conductor of the world's largest classroom through the revolutionary ten-week Eckhart Tolle webcast. Winfrey's daily journey into America's living rooms has created one of the incomparable brands in American history.

Stevie Wonder (b. 1950): Born in Saginaw, Michigan, Stevie Wonder has become a one-man cultural force, transforming pop music with his imagination, ingenuity, and soulfulness. Despite being blind from birth, Wonder has mastered a number of instruments as well as genres on his way to redefining the limits of twentieth-century soul, pop, R&B, and rock music.

At age twelve, Wonder was spotted by Motown producers and rechristened "Little Stevie Wonder" by founder Berry Gordy. Fame came easily to the young singer, who made his musical debut with the No. 1 hit single "Fingertips, Pt. 2," featuring a young Marvin Gaye on drums. He wrote and co-wrote hits throughout the mid-and late 1960s, including "The Tears of a Clown" for Smokey Robinson and the Miracles in 1967, and "I Was Made to Love Her" in 1967 and "For Once in My Life" in 1968, both of which reached No. 2 on the U.S. charts.

Turning from pop standards and show tunes to spiritual and political themes to electronic funk, Wonder produced five albums that are considered masterpieces: *Music of My Mind* (1972), *Talking Book* (1972), *Innervisions* (1973), *Fulfillingness' First Finale* (1974), and *Songs in the Key of Life* (1976). Wonder's revolutionary use of synthesizers, intricate and subtle melodic structures, socially conscious lyrics, and soulful vocals allowed him to break through every conceivable musical barrier. The musical genius has won twenty-six Grammy Awards in his career, as well as being inducted in the Rock and Roll Hall of Fame in 1989 and receiving the Kennedy Center Honors in 1999.

Tiger Woods (b. 1975): Born in Cypress, California, Eldrick "Tiger" Woods completely reordered the sports universe and became an international symbol for possibility. Woods, who is of mixed racial heritage, was an indisputable child prodigy, learning to play golf at age two. Between 1988 and 1991, he won the Junior World Golf Championship four consecutive years in a row, for a total of six wins in all.

Woods attended Stanford University and won numerous amateur U.S. golf titles, including the NCAA individual golf championship in 1996. Going pro that same year, he signed endorsement deals worth sixty-million dollars and was named *Sports Illustrated* Sportsman of the Year. The following year, Woods won the Masters, becoming the first African American to do so, as well as being the youngest—he was twenty-one.

Since 1997, he has won fourteen professional major golf championships, making him No. 2 on the all-time pro victories list. He is the youngest player to achieve the career Grand Slam and the youngest to win fifty tournaments on tour. Woods has been awarded the PGA Player of the Year Award nine times and named the Associated Press Male Athlete of the Year four times. *Forbes* magazine confirms that Woods is poised to become the world's first billionaire athlete by 2010. A major philanthropist, Woods has set up a number of charities, including The Tiger Woods Foundation, which offers a variety of services, including golf clinics aimed at underprivileged youth, and the off-season golf tournament he hosts, the Target World Challenge.

Richard Wright (1908–1960): Born in Roxie, Mississippi, Richard Wright survived his disadvantaged, impoverished youth to become one of twentieth-century America's literary heroes. At times controversial in his style and political leanings, Wright was one of the first African Americans to achieve broad literary fame.

Fleeing the South in 1927, Wright arrived in Chicago at the height of America's flirtation with communism and socialism. Like many young African Americans of his day, he internalized the solidarity rhetoric of the Left as a righteous critique of American racism. He began working on early drafts of his novels while writing and editing Communist Party newspapers during the Depression.

After a falling out with the local Communist Party, Wright relocated to New York City in 1937. Wright's literary career began with the publication of *Uncle Tom's Children* (1938), which gained him the fame and financial independence he needed to complete *Native Son* (1940). *Native Son* became an immediate bestseller and went on to be performed on Broadway.

Wright's legacy was assured. Often criticized for what many feared would be seen as playing into the fears of Whites, *Native Son* came to be seen as a major turning point in both American literature and race consciousness. By exposing the evils of White society to White society in a "real" way, Wright, in effect, birthed African American literature. His autobiography, *Black Boy*, was published in 1945, two years before Wright, feeling at odds with American political and cultural interests, permanently left America for France, where he remained for the rest of his life.

Whitney M. Young, Jr. (1921–1971): Born in Lincoln Ridge, Kentucky, Whitney Young rose to prominence as head of the National Urban League, rejuvenating the organization and pushing it to the forefront of the civil rights movement. After serving during World War II, Young earned his master's degree in social work from the University of Minnesota. It was there that he began volunteering with the St. Paul branch of the National Urban League. Founded in 1910, the National Urban League was created to help migrant African American workers make the transition to life in northern cities, but it had evolved little since the Great Migration early in the century. Young's success in Minnesota led him to serve as director of the Omaha, Nebraska, branch in 1950. Under his guidance, the Omaha chapter expanded its fight to secure equity in job hiring among Whites and Blacks, while its membership expanded threefold.

Throughout the 1950s, Young served in various executive positions fighting for African American civil rights, including a stint as the president of Georgia's NAACP. In 1961, at the age of forty, he was named president of the National Urban League. Seeing an organization in need of revitalization and new purpose, Young quickly redirected it toward the emerging civil rights movement. Leading the call for a "National Marshall Plan" to uplift America's poor, Young's leadership gained him access to Presidents Kennedy, Johnson, and Nixon, while drastically increasing the institutional capacity of the National Urban League for all time. In 1969, President Johnson awarded Young the Presidential Medal of Freedom.

Acknowledgments

GRATEFUL ACKNOWLEDGMENT IS MADE TO EACH OF THE
AMERICA I AM LEGENDS, WHOSE EXTRAORDINARY LIVES
AND ACCOMPLISHMENTS MADE THIS AMAZING JOURNEY POSSIBLE.

Very special thanks to our Legends Team, whose heads, hearts, and hands joined together to demonstrate love and service in action.

Nona Gaye, the Gaye Family, and Bona Justitia Music, Inc. for generously allowing us to present Marvin Gaye's portrait on the cover of this book.

Tavis Smiley, for the gift of America I AM: The African American Imprint.

Reid Tracy for his ongoing support.

Denise Pines who planted the original golden seeds for this project.

Cheryl Woodruff, who held the creative vision, rolled up her sleeves, and refused to stop until we crossed the finish line.

Juan Roberts, our brilliant designer, whose exceptional artistry and unsurpassed dedication brought each Legend to new life.

Colby Hamilton, our Legends MVP, who played every position with intelligence, resourcefulness, and heart.

Diana Marie Delgado for being a crucial pillar of support during this entire process.

Carolyn Fowler and Debi Rose Catalano for wise counsel.

The Global PSD Staff: Steven Goff, Gina Chiu, and Erik Ko for producing such a beautiful book.

Cheryll Greene, Rich Remsberg, Heather Hart, Muriel Jorgensen, Robert Fleming, Clarence Reynolds, Carl Arnold, Lisa Reece, Christy Salinas, and Jill Kramer for their generous contributions to this project.

INDEX

(Entries in italics indicate subject quotation source)

We hoped you enjoyed this SMILEYBOOKS publication.
If you would like to receive additional information, please contact:

SMILEYBOOKS

33 West 19th Street, 4th Floor
New York, New York, 10011

Distributed by:

Hay House, Inc.
P.O. Box 5100
Carlsbad, CA 92018-5100

(760) 431-7695 or (800) 654-5126
(760) 431-6948 (fax) or (800) 650-5115 (fax)
www.hayhouse.com® • www.hayfoundation.org

***

Published and distributed in Australia by: Hay House Australia Pty. Ltd. • 18/36 Ralph St. •
Alexandria NSW 2015 • Phone: 612-9669-4299 • Fax: 612-9669-4144 • www.hayhouse.com.au

Published and distributed in the United Kingdom by: Hay House UK, Ltd. • 292B Kensal Rd.,
London W10 5BE • Phone: 44-20-8962-1230 • Fax: 44-20-8962-1239 • www.hayhouse.co.uk

Published and distributed in the Republic of South Africa by: Hay House SA (Pty), Ltd., P.O.
Box 990, Witkoppen 2068 • Phone/Fax: 27-11-467-8904 • orders@psdprom.co.za •
www.hayhouse.co.za

Published and Distributed in India by: Hay House Publishers India, Muskaan Complex, Plot No.
3, B-2, Vasant Kunj, New Delhi 110 070 • Phone: 91-11-4176-1620 • Fax: 91-11-4176-1630 •
www.hayhouse.co.in

Distributed in Canada by: Raincoast • 9050 Shaughnessy St., Vancouver, B.C. V6P 6E5 •
Phone: (604) 323-7100 • Fax: (604) 323-2600